Acquisitions in the New Information Universe

Core Competencies and Ethical Practices

JESSE HOLDEN

Neal-Schuman Publishers, Inc.

New York   London

Published by Neal-Schuman Publishers, Inc.
100 William St., Suite 2004
New York, NY 10038

Printed and bound in the United States of America.

The paper used in this publication meets the minimum requirements of American National Standard for Information Sciences–Permanence of Paper for Printed Library Materials, ANSI Z39.48-1992.

Library of Congress Cataloging-in-Publication Data

Holden, Jesse.
    Acquisitions in the new information universe : core competencies and ethical practices / Jesse Holden.
        p. cm.
    Includes bibliographical references and index.
    ISBN 978-1-55570-696-8 (alk. paper)
    1. Acquisitions (Libraries) 2. Acquisition of electronic information resources. 3. Libraries and electronic publishing. 4. Acquisitions (Libraries)—Technological innovations. 5. Acquisitions (Libraries)—Moral and ethical aspects. 6. Acquisitions librarians—Professional ethics. I. Title.

Z689.H74 2010
025.2—dc22
                                                                    2010000228

This book is dedicated to

Elizabeth,
for her support,

Elliot,
for his patience,

and

Adelaide,
whose father has been writing this book
since before she was born.

Contents

List of Figures

Preface

Recent changes in libraries, along with a parallel shift in librarianship, have done nothing short of redefining the traditional role of libraries in society. The fundamental role of the library has shifted from warehousing a limited quantity of information to filtering and providing access to the seemingly infinite amount of information available today.

As the nature of library collections has changed, so, too, has the nature of library acquisitions. Many legacy acquisitions workflows are organized around creating, tracking, buying, receiving, and filing paper items. As the unit of the library that was once primarily responsible for gathering together the physical materials that would create the library's collection, the definition of acquisitions of library material has inevitably changed alongside other aspects of librarianship.

From an item-driven process concerned almost entirely with the physical containers of information—books, journals, DVDs, and so on—acquisitions has become increasingly involved with the provision of access to content in a variety of formats, including resources that might once have been considered outside the scope of the library's collection. Though paper will be a part of libraries for the foreseeable future, there is a clear movement away from paper-based information sources and records management toward electronic content and content management. Despite this shift, acquisitions has received relatively little systematic attention; it has remained a largely reactive part of librarianship. Work in this subdiscipline of librarianship has mostly focused on incorporating new developments into existing models.

With the transformational shift in focus from item to format, the mission of acquisitions has changed from acquiring things to connecting with content. This has transformed the process of acquisitions from one that is reactive to one that is proactive. No longer defined by, nor confined to, the technical act of procurement, or buying things outright, acquisitions has come to encompass many responsibilities that could not be accommodated by an earlier paradigm of librarianship. To connect patrons with the content that they need at a time when they need it, including the distant future, acquisitions practitioners must act quickly, strategically, and efficiently.

Acquisitions in the New Information Universe: Core Competencies and Ethical Practices is conceived primarily as a concept-based approach to acquisitions for both new and experienced acquisitions professionals. This book will help orient those who are unfamiliar with acquisitions to the profession, while providing a new lens for experienced professionals to (re)conceptualize their daily work. In all cases, the approach presented here is designed to be a point of departure for engaging the challenges and possibilities inherent in contemporary acquisitions work. The work is organized to introduce key ideas and emphasizes strategic approaches for practicing acquisitions holistically in the contemporary information environment.

The chapters that follow cover key traditional acquisitions concepts like ordering, receiving, dealing with licenses, and using integrated library systems and online vendor databases in an acquisitions workflow. However, the primary objective is to integrate these concepts according to a new model emphasizing the role that acquisitions plays in overall library *access* and *service* in addition to *procurement*. In other words, the new model discussed in the following chapters is intended to be one that is responsive and adaptive to the unforeseen, yet inevitable, changes in acquisitions.

Acquisitions in the New Information Universe: Core Competencies and Ethical Practices seeks to achieve three goals. First is the presentation of a comprehensive introduction for those who are new to acquisitions, one that reflects the nature of the information with which they work. Since many practitioners find themselves working in acquisitions purely by chance, this text will serve as a guide for those looking for current information on acquisitions. The second goal is to establish a new, relevant conceptual approach to acquisitions practice that comprehensively systematizes contemporary acquisitions work in a holistic way. This new framework will be valuable to new and experienced library practitioners working in acquisitions or other areas of content management. Finally, this work will provide a basis for defining the continuing role of acquisitions practice, both as its own subdiscipline of librarianship and as the role of acquisitions within the context of the library.

Chapter 1 orients the acquisitions practitioner within this new information universe, specifically the universe created through academic publishing and other scholarly communication, by discussing a model that could be used to frame contemporary acquisitions functions. Chapter 2 develops the idea of "spheres of access" within the context of strategically rethinking the nature of acquisitions. Chapter 3 builds on the idea of "access" as it relates to acquisitions by investigating the paths available to the acquisitions practitioner. Chapter 4 complements the acquisition of content with the service and feedback aspects of acquisitions work, specifically as it has emerged in contemporary practice. Finally, Chapter 5 looks ahead to a possible future of acquisitions shaped by a forward-looking acquisitions practice.

Readers will notice that the theme throughout is one of appropriating and providing access to information rather than establishing fixed workflows designed around handling rigid categories of materials.

Much of what is written about acquisitions, especially in the journal literature, is focused on the academic library environment. The primary reason for this is that the pressures and opportunities within scholarly communication have created a state of constant flux. *Acquisitions in the New Information Universe: Core Competencies and Ethical Practices* is designed for a range of library types and sizes. Midsized and large academic libraries with discrete and autonomous acquisitions units will recognize their operations throughout. Library science students who are interested in the transformative changes brought about by technology and user-centered service approaches within the context of technical services will benefit from the framework outlined in the text. Small academic libraries will be able to incorporate many of these concepts into existing procedures. Public libraries will be able to draw from this model, especially in the provision of access to licensed electronic resources. The model in the chapters that follow provides a strategic basis for a contemporary practice of library content acquisitions in any setting.

After completing the book, readers will have an overview of core competencies and corresponding strategies for dealing with common issues in daily acquisitions work while developing a new overarching conceptual framework for considering acquisitions processes and goals. Importantly, ethical practices emphasized throughout should significantly inform how those operations are carried out on a day-to-day basis.

Acknowledgments

I think that acquisitions is the most interesting profession in the world, and I owe that perspective mostly to the people with whom I have had the privilege of working over the years. I would thank everyone by name if I could, but the result would be a text substantially longer than the one before you. I will therefore have to settle for a general, though no less sincere, thanks to those with whom I have worked in the Stanford Law Library Technical Services division, the Stanford University Libraries acquisitions department, the Millersville University Library, and the ALCTS "Fundamentals" courses. None of what follows would have been possible without having been surrounded by these amazing colleagues.

I would like to single out a few individuals who made this specific text possible.

Regina Wallen first hired me as Acquisitions Manager and empowered me to set up an acquisitions unit that was goal oriented rather than process based. That approach has informed all the work I have done in acquisitions and those lessons permeate this text.

Sharon Propas has been a long-time mentor, friend, and interlocutor about many things, both acquisitions and otherwise. Sharon understands acquisitions in a way that few others do and has helped me in ways that few others could. In addition to years of invaluable professional advice, I owe her many thanks for her feedback and insights on early drafts of both this text and the concepts on which it is based.

Carol Lawrence has enthusiastically supported my work from the beginning. Carol for years made the Integrated Library System and payments systems intelligible to me and solved many vexing technical quandaries that I could not have escaped on my own.

Marjorie Warmkessel's support for and conversations about this project have kept me enthused, confident, and moving forward. I am especially grateful for her careful readings of and insightful comments about my later drafts of this text.

Greg Seigworth, besides being a good friend, is, as luck would have it, an expert on Deleuzian philosophy. Greg thoughtfully reviewed some of this text despite facing important deadlines of his own.

Scott Anderson and Marilyn Parrish acted as sounding boards as I worked out some of the more conceptual ideas in this text. Erin Dorney provided much-needed assistance with Adobe Illustrator as I struggled to get the graphics for this text production ready.

Rick Anderson and Katina Strauch have worked diligently to transform acquisitions. Rick, in challenging many long-held assumptions and practices, has pioneered new approaches to acquisitions and made some once-radical ideas generally acceptable. Katina, through her leadership of the annual Charleston conference, "Issues in Book and Serials Acquisition," and editorship of *Against the Grain*, has facilitated critical dialogue among the acquisitions, collection development, publishing, and vending communities. She has been a true agent of change and inspiration in the profession.

Finally, I would like to thank my editors at Neal-Schuman, Paul Seeman, Sandy Wood, and Amy Knauer, who helped me develop, refine, and ultimately finish this text. I would also like to thank Charles Harmon for his support of this project.

Despite the many expert opinions that were willingly shared with me throughout the writing and revision process, mistakes in my text and inadequacies in the model are all my own.

Thanks, everyone!

Chapter 1

The New Information Universe

The Information Age

With the invention of desktop computing and the subsequent launch of the Internet, the world found itself taking its first uncertain steps into the information age. While time has tempered enthusiasm for the widespread use of the Internet and experience has diminished people's expectations for the maturing technology, it is an undeniable truism that information technology has had a profound, even revolutionary, effect on research and scholarly communication. The emerging practices within academe over the last fifteen years were not conceivable before the advent of the World Wide Web. Clearly, the promise of transformation, though not utopian by any means, has delivered a significant amount of change in a relatively short time.

The library, as a dynamic hub of scholarly communication, has likewise undergone profound changes. These transformative changes have affected not only information but the entire information environment (Pritchard, 2008). As a critical nexus within the information universe, the library functions as both a lens through which these changes can be examined and a mirror in which change can be reflected. If the library, then, is an

1

instrument through which the transition to the information age can be at once observed and traced, it is critical for the contemporary information practitioner to fully understand the role that the library now plays as well as the potential future roles that it might yet play. Within the library itself, it is imperative that those individuals who secure access to selected information—that is, those individuals that practice acquisitions—understand the instabilities that exist in this new information universe in terms of production, distribution, and, especially, access.

But if we have arrived in an "information age," what does that mean? If it is important to fix the emergence of contemporary acquisitions practice, like all library practice today, within the field of a nascent information age, then this common yet ambiguous term must be more carefully defined. Though the boundaries of an "age" may seem arbitrary, or at the very least debatable, such a designation is not merely a convenient way of breaking up history for the sake of study. "Ages" are useful because they encapsulate paradigms, or systems of perception and thought. Such an approach to conceiving of change in the information universe as successive, independent historical frames is informed by two important concepts. The first is Michel Foucault's "archaeological" perspective of history. Within this frame of reference, there are, internal to each particular discourse, periods when knowledge is organized in a logical way. The resulting discursive strata, then, are marked off by a "profound breach in the expanse of continuities" (Foucault, 1994: 217), a moment when the internal logic changes. In this "radical event, ... things are no longer perceived, describe[d], expressed, characterized, and classified in the same way" (Foucault, 1994: 217). Significantly, the divisions between strata are neither so many arbitrary marks in a continuous flow of passing time nor a teleological advance of a conveniently compartmentalized historical totality. Library practice in the information age, for example, is just one of many contemporary discourses arranged according to a relative logic, inherently different from the library practice of the preceding age. However, it is also important to note that it is also distinct from other discourses of the age, though closely related to many of them.

A second useful, parallel concept for conceiving of such a radical break is presented in Thomas Kuhn's (1996) view of a "paradigm shift," fundamental to his notion of scientific revolutions. Rather than assuming a continuous and even development of scientific thought and discovery, Kuhn theorizes that a shift in paradigm is the result of a crisis—specifically, the inability of the former, accepted paradigm to explain what is being observed. At the point the established paradigm loses its explanatory power, a new paradigm must be defined to account for the emerging anomalies. Therefore, when considering a model for acquisitions, the emerging practices and information technologies used in research, publication, and dissemination of information mark a situation that can no longer be adequately addressed by an existing paradigm and signal that the time has come for a paradigm shift.

The implications for the practice of acquisitions are great. Specifically, contemporary practice implies a Foucauldian discourse about context that is *specific to* and *contained in* the historical field in which it emerges and a Kuhnian view that paradigm change is *contiguous* rather than *continuous*. If the information environment has experienced a recent shift rather than a gradual evolution, what does such a change mean for acquisitions practice? Quite simply, the time has come to "radicalize" acquisitions—that is, to rethink what it means to "do acquisitions" today and how that work is to be done. Acquisitions must be based on contemporary reality rather than the continuation of past practices. Realignment of acquisitions, therefore, requires rethinking the entire approach to the function rather than adjusting parts of existing workflows to accommodate innovations in scholarly communication and academic practice.

Paradigm Shift

This shift in paradigm—the shift to a new age of information—begs the simple question: What is information? For the sake of the following discussion, the simple answer is that it can be almost anything. Information is anything that can be known. With such a general definition, it is important to keep in mind that the hallmark of the age is the relative abundance and presumed availability of information, along with the assumption that most information can be accessed from almost anywhere whenever it is needed. The production and communication of information that underlies the paradigm shift to the information age does not, however, imply a corresponding increase in quality or meaning of that information. In other words, more is not necessarily better. Because of that, any work with information becomes only more complex, contextualized, and specialized. It is also worth noting that despite the vast amount of accessible information, some information will remain strictly localized.

Several concepts are particularly important to clarify before proceeding with the kind of rethinking or "re-visioning" of acquisitions that is needed to enhance and support the changed role of the academic library in the new age. These terms are "information," "content," "format," "access," and "feedback." The last three terms are addressed in some detail in the following chapters. However, while all the terms impact the concept of the information universe, the *idea of* and *distinction between* "information" and "content" is critical for establishing a meaningful dialogue. These slippery terms have become increasingly useless during the rapid rise and fall of various Internet trends. In general usage, both *content* and *information* are at once in danger of becoming synonymous or meaningless—or both. In the pages that follow, these two terms are used in different and deliberate ways.

Within the context of libraries, and especially acquisitions, we are concerned with what can be both known and communicated.

While communicability is not inherent to information, it is obviously necessary for library-based information practice. Anything that can be communicated can also be contained—in a book, a database, a transmission, or a language—so when describing information that can be communicated, this class of information will be referred to as "content." This is an important distinction in moving the dialogue forward because it is a direct refutation of some contemporary ideas about information. Often there is a perception that information is ethereal, all around us yet not tangible. For example, Electronic Frontier Foundation (EFF) cofounder John Perry Barlow asserts that information "isn't a noun," "a thing," or "an object" (Barlow, 2008: xvi), an interpretation that is misleading when in many instances, including librarianship, information is being treated as such in a practical, commodified way. Information is, in fact, all three of those things—noun, thing, *and* object; and that is a critical point for acquisitions practitioners to be well aware of. It is true that information is so abundant, pervasive, and seemingly accessible that it often lacks inherent meaning of its own. The meaning comes from the context in which the information is situated and the use that is subsequently made of it. While "content" will foremost describe *communicability*, information that has become content will also imply a minimum level of *organization*, too. This further distinguishes content, information that is useful and available, from the rest of the vast, chaotic, and ever-expanding information universe.

Though information has always been important, what makes this new age so different is the incredible ubiquity of information. The combination of technology, perception, and practice that constitutes our new paradigm and differentiates it from those that preceded it is the shift from *information scarcity* to *information abundance*. The latter is reflected not only in the absolute volume of information but in the associated uncertainty that such abundance generates (Winseck, 2002). The work of contemporary libraries, therefore, is largely concerned with *filtering* all of the available information in order to provide a specific path to *only* that content that is useful in a given circumstance. While this filtering function is not in itself a complete break with past library practice, the emphasis on having or getting information has been superseded with a more conditional function of *connecting*. A direct result of this shift in paradigm—impacting library function and user expectation—is that the mechanisms developed over time to address the past problem of scarcity are likely to be irrelevant, both to the library professional working with the information and the user who is looking for it (Anderson, 2007).

Such a change has profound implications for the practice of acquisitions. If the traditional conception of acquisitions has been getting information—that is, building a collection—it follows that acquisitions work is especially sensitive to changes in the information environment in which it functions. Of course, the whole library is situated within the broader regime of information production and distribution that has likewise changed, but acquisitions has a primary responsibility for linking the library to the broader information universe beyond the immediate library community. Work with publishers, vendors, and accounting departments links acquisitions to a unique and essential part of that broader information universe. This link beyond the library's sphere to the universe of information remains a key function of acquisitions, but in a way that is becoming more complex yet less defined. The need for acquisitions practitioners who are highly skilled information professionals is becoming acute since many of the responsibilities in acquisitions require a multifaceted, technologically charged strategic approach to achieve success.

Any description of an "information universe" will be at best reflective of the moment in time at which such a description is made. While there has always been an information universe, its makeup has varied by location (geographic, social, and temporal), content (what is known, what is possible to know, and what is communicated), and technology (both technologies of inscription and technologies of dissemination). The content and usage of this universe are always affected by cultural and perceptual contingency. While the academic library predates the Internet, the contemporary praxis of academic librarianship is entirely enmeshed in a system of information that is driven by the Internet. It would be difficult for anyone working in libraries today to imagine their work without, at the very least, the World Wide Web. Internet resources have expanded at such a rate and with such versatile functionality as to crowd out other kinds of resources, such as CD-ROMs, magnetic diskettes, and even microfilm. For the sake of practicality, one should not anchor one's conception of acquisitions work in a time before the Internet existed. In terms of information production, distribution, and use, the invention of personal computing and subsequent launch of the Internet led to a paradigm shift of the highest magnitude.

What has become problematic in the wake of this paradigm shift, though, is the tendency to treat any information in an electronic form as a kind of add-on to the acquisitions processes already in place for physical items. In many cases this has resulted in approaching, or trying to approach, all information as *items*, like books, instead of treating books as just one type of information entity. What needs to occur for acquisitions to (re)position itself within the (new) information universe along with other areas of librarianship, such as cataloging and metadata or reference and information services, is not so much for acquisitions practitioners to learn more than they already do, but to rethink what they already know. For those just starting within the professional practice of acquisitions, it is important to learn an approach that is open and flexible in order to account for the plethora of information situations. In either case, it is equally essential that the universe in which they will be working is presented and organized in such a way that their practices make sense.

A Functional Model of Acquisitions

The reconception of acquisitions may take a cue from the substantial effort put toward the Functional Requirements for Bibliographic Records (FRBR) model developed within the cataloging community. This "conceptual model for the bibliographic universe" (Tillett, 2004) generalizes bibliographic entities, their creators, and the relationship between the two. This model has generated significant debate in the profession and has profound implications for restructuring both the *approach to* and *practice of* cataloging. Though the outcomes of this discussion are far from certain, the concepts and the conversation have nonetheless informed a kind of reflexive reevaluation of the purpose and practice of cataloging. As the changing nature of information production and its subsequent communication have precipitated a reevaluation of the idea of cataloging practice, so too should it likewise affect the *approach to* and *practice of* the acquisition of library content. What we see within librarianship is the shift from a modern to a truly postmodern praxis that must be marked by a simultaneous change in thought as well as practice.

Of course, the Internet—and the Web in particular—is the primary driver behind this change and, as such, it is easy to see the Net as either a panacea or pariah. But this is not to say that everything that matters is available online, nor to advocate that it should be. This is likewise not to suggest that physical materials across a variety of media are no longer relevant or should no longer be considered content for use by and within the scholarly community. However, when looking at information qua content vis-à-vis the library and how it is handled by acquisitions, what becomes critical in the execution and evaluation of practice is the premise that the Internet is a de facto part of the environment rather than an afterthought or a supplement. The implication for practice in an information universe premised on the existence and, more importantly, the general acceptance of online and other digital media is that any practices must necessarily be built with the understanding that online media will be a critical part of that universe.

One of the undeniable trends of the Internet age is the increased sensitivity to access. "Access" may be defined broadly as the ability to consume specific information, but should not necessarily be constrained by a notion of *immediacy*. In other words, access is best interpreted broadly: it does not mean that everything need be immediately accessible on demand or that all demands for content must be immediately filled. The issues surrounding access have burgeoned from the straightforward act of *finding* information to the more nuanced and complicated contemporary regime of copyright, so-called digital rights management (DRM), and the sheer amount of information, useful or not, that can be retrieved from even the most basic of Web searches. The overwhelming intricacies of access in the rapidly maturing information age have necessarily repositioned the information professional well within this regime.

It would be a mistake, however, to approach twenty-first-century acquisitions from the point of view of access alone. Though it was recognized some time ago that "acquisitions will be redefined in terms of access" (Gorman, 1997: xiii, paraphrasing Cornish, 1997), only recently is it becoming clear exactly what that means. Cornish (1997), for his part, conceives of access in terms of how content is *funded* by the library rather than how it is *appropriated* for use. In Cornish's approach, content should only be acquired if it is within the scope of a given collection. What has emerged since this model was put forward is a regime in which the line between what exactly *is* or *is not* the library collection can be difficult to draw definitively.

Lee (2000: 1111), for example, making note of the changing nature of what constitutes a *collection*, has suggested that "given the new reality… it would be beneficial to broaden the concept of the collection to reflect the continuity and interconnectivity characteristic" of the contemporary information environment.

For Lee, like many librarians, the idea of the collection cannot necessarily be conveniently defined or limited by what is "owned" (see Chapter 2). Anderson (2006) has gone so far as to suggest moving away from a permanent *just-in-case* collection in favor of *just-in-time* acquisitions in those cases where such a model better meets library user needs; he has recently emphasized the possibility to reorganize collection development around the emerging ability to respond to library user demand by "showing our patrons everything that's available and buying only what they need" (2009: 86). Clearly the idea of access to content that is driven primarily—or even entirely—by real-time demand is significant for the practice of acquisitions, as it signals an important shift from *building a general collection*, a linear process, to more precisely *meeting specific needs* at the point they arise, something altogether different and much less straightforward. In the ontological realignment that underpins the whole paradigm shift, even the priority of the collection within the library's organization scheme, long taken for granted, is fundamentally called into question.

Conclusion: A Call for Radicalization

The information universe is a priori an ever-expanding one. Information (and content) is being constantly created and reorganized. The time has passed when those practicing acquisitions can wait for a stack of paper orders and buy a bunch of books. The information matrix within which we all work seems, at times, hopelessly complicated. Acquisitions in the new information universe requires a detailed understanding of not just *where* something is available but *how*. Embedded in this understanding is a new kind of competency in dealing with information as a granular abstract rather than merely an aggregate of things or "stuff" to be bought and bar coded.

Goldsborough notes that "today, in the Information Age, we typically think of ourselves as uniquely inundated with information"

(2002: 15). His suggestion for managing inundation includes automated filtering functions. However, even with the advances in technology-driven information searching—a process that has, in practice, already become de facto filtering—the importance of human input is still recognized. Marwick maintains that "it is important to note that knowledge management problems can typically not be solved by the deployment of a technology solution alone" (2001: 816). Navigating the information universe is complex in that it requires maximizing resources in a way that simultaneously *expands* and *narrows* the available content that is required by an end user by distilling the most useful content from the broadest number of information sources. This pull in equal but opposite directions poses a direct challenge to anyone supporting and providing information services, as it requires a generalization of the information universe while demanding a nuanced understanding of that ever-larger body of potentially accessible information.

Acquisitions practices have developed by addressing change in a gradual, evolutionary manner, contrary to the nature of paradigm shift. Praxis has morphed more by the accretion of exceptions within the acquisitions function than from deliberate engagement with the fundamental paradigm shift affecting the wider information universe. In order to address this shift, tools and techniques must be derived from current needs and opportunities rather than appended to those practices that arose within the previous age. While defying a formal prescription for specific practice, the new frame of reference for finding and delivering content requires a radicalization of approach rather than simply adding or updating particular actions in an already-fixed workflow. Acquisitions workflows and practices built upon this former approach will be more likely to succeed and adapt in the destabilized information environment in which contemporary librarianship is practiced. Overcoming this inertia requires a comprehensive conceptual approach that addresses, rather than accommodates, these profound changes.

References

Anderson, Rick. 2006. "Crazy Idea #274: Just Stop Collecting." *Against the Grain* 18, no. 4: 50–52.

Anderson, Rick. 2007. "It's Not about the Workflow: Patron-Centered Practices for 21st-Century Serialists." *The Serials Librarian* 51, no. 3/4: 189–199.

Anderson, Rick. 2009. "Is the Library Collection Too Risky?" *Against the Grain* 21, no. 3: 86.

Barlow, John Perry. 2008. "Foreword." In *Content: Selected Essays on Technology, Creativity, and the Future of the Future* (pp. xv–xxii), by Cory Doctorow. San Francisco: Tachyon.

Cornish, Graham P. 1997. "Electronic Document Delivery Services and Their Impact on Collection Management." In *Collection Management for the 21st Century: A Handbook for Librarians* (pp. 159–172), edited by G. E. Gorman and Ruth H. Miller. Westport, CT: Greenwood Press.

Foucault, Michel. 1994. *The Order of Things: An Archaeology of the Human Sciences*. New York: Vintage Books.

Goldsborough, Reid. 2002. "Breaking the Information Logjam." *Reading Today* 20, no. 1 (Aug./Sept.): 15.

Gorman, G. E. 1997. "Introduction." In *Collection Management for the 21st Century: A Handbook for Librarians* (pp. ix–xv), edited by G. E. Gorman and Ruth H. Miller. Westport, CT: Greenwood Press.

Kuhn, Thomas S. 1996. *The Structure of Scientific Revolutions*, 3rd ed. Chicago: University of Chicago Press.

Lee, Hur-Li. 2000. "What Is a Collection?" *Journal of the American Society for Information Science* 52, no. 12: 1106–1113.

Marwick, A. D. 2001. "Knowledge Management and Technology." *IBM Systems Journal* 40, no. 4: 814–830.

Pritchard, Sarah M. 2008. "Deconstructing the Library: Reconceptualizing Collections, Spaces and Services." *Journal of Library Administration* 48, no. 2: 219–233.

Tillett, Barbara. 2004. *What Is FRBR? A Conceptual Model for the Bibliographic Universe*. Washington, DC: Library of Congress Cataloging Distribution Service. Available: www.loc.gov/cds/downloads/FRBR.PDF (accessed November 23, 2009).

Winseck, Dwayne. 2002. "Illusions of Perfect Information and Fantasies of Control in the Information Society." *New Media and Society* 4, no. 1: 93–122.

Chapter 2

Spheres of Access

The Changing Nature of Acquisitions

With the rapid advance of computing technology leading to the Internet and the widespread adoption of the Web as the ubiquitous medium of the information age, all stakeholders in the production-dissemination processes of scholarly communication—authors, publishers, vendors, and libraries—have faced considerable upheaval in traditional processes. Many libraries have already moved beyond models of acquisitions that are centered on print (Carr, 2008). While sorting out how this shift has affected, and continues to affect, libraries, a basic question needs to be asked: What is acquisitions? And how has that upheaval shaped the functions of acquisitions today?

Collecting materials *for* and *within* libraries has been a basic part of librarianship from the profession's inception. Indeed, libraries have been associated with their physical collections going back to ancient times. Long defined primarily by their collections, libraries have depended on the process of getting materials into the collection in an organized, efficient way. Yet, despite the obvious necessity of acquiring materials that constitute the collection, acquisitions—both as a distinct unit and as a collective set of processes—is often taken for granted. When

---

Selection and Acquisition

A library user wants to recommend a title for purchase. Using the library's Web directory, the user contacts someone in the acquisitions unit, assuming that the acquisitions staff is responsible for making content decisions in addition to ordering and receiving content. What happens now?

People often assume that acquisitions involves the complete cycle of identifying, selecting, ordering, and paying for the content that library users have access to. Really, content acquisition is just the second part of the content development process, and its related tasks are usually performed by an individual or unit other than the one doing the selecting.

In the case of a user-initiated request, someone responsible for content decisions would need to review and approve the request regardless of who was first contacted. Those performing a task traditionally regarded as collection development use a number of factors to make the decision to acquire content. Factors likely include the library's collection development policy and its mission, access issues, and available funding. Once collection development has

(Continued on facing page)

---

acquisitions is considered, it tends to be misunderstood—even by other librarians. The business aspects of library budgets, for-profit vendors, and financial record keeping are unfamiliar, perhaps even intimidating, to librarians who are not engaged with acquisitions work on a daily basis. As the information universe becomes more complex, both in the amount and potential availability of information, so, too, does the role that acquisitions plays in the library and in scholarly communication generally.

Part of the confusion stems from the position of acquisitions in the library vis-à-vis other units. On the one hand, acquisitions does not have an equivalent set of national-level rules such as cataloging librarians use to structure their work. This can

---

Selection and Acquisition *(Continued)*

authorized and assigned a funding source, the request will be
forwarded to acquisitions to be ordered.

Often, the order will come through to acquisitions with a
suggestion of where to buy the content, such as a local bookstore or
popular online vendor. While such recommendations can be helpful
in the case of rare or other difficult-to-obtain content, the acquisitions
practitioner is usually in the best position to make sourcing decisions.
A number of factors are involved in deciding from where to source
content, including potential discounts, shipping options and costs,
and processing services. The evaluation and selection of content
suppliers is one of the key strategic functions for acquisitions.

While costs are an important factor, it is important that any
decision about a vendor takes into account the services available.
Such services could include designated representatives, approval
plans, standing orders, or anything else that makes the process of
acquisitions easier and more efficient. In the same way that collection
development makes strategic decisions about what content is
appropriate to provide through the library, acquisitions makes
analogous decisions about how the content is obtained.

---

make it more difficult to define the scope and competencies of
acquisitions work. On the other hand, as a "technical service,"
acquisitions has not had the same exposure to and interaction
with library users as more public-facing library units. While,
again, the library must necessarily secure access rights to content
so that the library users may, in turn, use that content, most
users do not give the acquisitions process any thought as long as
they are able to find the information that they are seeking. In
truth, library users should not have to think about how content
is made available, but such a seamless provision of information
is becoming increasingly hard to accomplish since this content
is provided through many routes. Additionally, users may have
significant experience using commercial Web search engines,

music download services, and streaming video, and so are not accustomed to waiting for information delivery.

The other part of the confusion comes from the changing nature of acquisitions itself: the tools used, methods employed, content sought, and, not least of all, the access required. Acquisitions practitioners from a previous age would hardly recognize much of what is done in acquisitions today as a matter of routine. Or, rather, they would not recognize *how* it is done. The paradigm shift from a stable, print-based information universe to one that includes electronic media has created an environment of permanent flux within acquisitions, just as that permanent flux now permeates the whole library environment. We are well into the postmodern age when "new formats, new economic realities, and new expectations from our communities will ensure that we will be required to change often from now on" (Propas and Reich, 1995: 46). The recent rise of electronic journal packages, academic e-books, streaming media, and various associated pricing models for these new, Web-based resources underscores the instability inherent to the information age. The flux within acquisitions is so constant now as to be an integral condition of the work, to such a degree that the goal of the acquisitions function is to reach a kind of *equilibrium* rather than *stability*.

Challenging the notion of a stable and orderly information universe are the contingencies that come along with processing e-resources. Acquisitions practitioners might be involved in reviewing licensing agreements, setting up online access with a publisher, and responding to service outages in addition to more traditional acquisitions functions. Given the unique nature of many e-content products, associated access management issues can be very time consuming. Because access is so directly tied to the acquisition process, those involved with acquisitions may be more closely tied to ongoing access than ever before. On top of it all, most libraries will need to maintain

Stability versus Equilibrium

While stability might have seemed a possibility—or even the ultimate goal—in the universe of printed content, it is not a realistic goal for the new information universe. The challenging factors that come along with e-resources, like multiple pricing models, publisher-specific licenses, and various access options, are simply overwhelming. At the same time, this dynamic environment provides new kinds of opportunities.

Along with additional steps necessary to shepherd e-content through the acquisitions and access processes, technology may also provide some critical time-saving solutions. Options for electronically delivered invoices, the provision of machine-readable cataloging (MARC) record files, and customizable usage statistics may make the trade-off not only worthwhile, but even advantageous. Though it may not be possible to establish the same kind of regular workflow that could be achieved with an item-based acquisitions program, new technology-based services can allow acquisitions practitioners to recoup some of the time needed for acquiring e-resources. Knowing and leveraging the available service options from publishers and vendors is an important part of using time strategically.

For example, the time taken to negotiate and set up access to a large e-journal package might be somewhat offset in the long run by having publisher-supplied MARC records—if the records did not require significant editing in-house—and automated usage statistics that replace an in-house system requiring manual manipulation. It is important to note, though, that any time saved may be on the institutional level and not necessarily in acquisitions.

a simultaneous workflow for print and other physical-format resources as well.

One way of dealing with this destabilization in the information environment is to move away from rigid workflows, especially those based on assumptions or traditional practices. While processes in acquisitions have tended to be formulated in terms of linear and concrete steps that were presumed to include all potential items that could be added to a collection, such practices may no longer be effective when dealing with the challenges emerging in the contemporary information environment. Reformulating workflow in terms of the shared goals or ideals of the library, particularly concerning potential and intended access, acquisitions will operate with more flexibility, intention, and relevance. While predetermined workflows will still be required to process certain kinds of content in some cases, a successful acquisitions strategy will not be premised on the assumption that all content can be treated in a uniform manner. This is especially the case when an acquisitions program involves many formats (see discussion in Chapter 3).

However, while many changes have impacted—and continue to impact—acquisitions, the core responsibilities have stayed basically the same. An acquisitions professional's responsibilities will likely include verification and sourcing of selected content (including format options, price, and availability), placing orders and encumbering associated funds, following up on unfulfilled orders (including claiming or canceling orders), receiving materials or establishing access to online content, paying invoices, and monitoring the library's acquisitions budget. Much of the fundamental confusion related to the changing nature of acquisitions originates with that initial misunderstanding of its basic role, stemming in part from the localized nature of the practices established to fulfill these responsibilities. Acquisitions, with its traditional focus almost entirely on the *item*, is a hybrid of library functions; being neither entirely process-based nor entirely content-based, it occupies a unique place within the library, which is further elaborated on in Chapter 4.

Besides the core responsibilities, the ethics of acquisitions remain a foundation upon which any sound assemblage of acquisitions practice must be predicated. Ethics may be defined specifically in this context as "the principles of conduct governing an individual or a group," but can also be considered more broadly as "a theory or system of moral values" or simply as "a guiding philosophy" (Merriam-Webster Online). Acquisitions practice is multifaceted and may include *service, business, supervision,* or *scholarship.* With the shifts in both the informational and economic environments in which acquisitions functions, the understanding, articulation, and practice of ethics within daily work and strategic planning is more crucial than ever. Tightening budgets coupled with the explosion of desirable content requires the deliberate engagement with and discussion about ethics as they relate to all interactions and transactions. A critical guide for any practitioner of acquisitions is the "Statement on Principles and Standards of Acquisitions Practice" (see sidebar on following page).

One long-standing assumption about the information universe that must be reconsidered is the notion of the supply chains that operate within it. Supply of information to or within the library has traditionally been thought of in terms of linear models. Information flowing into the library has followed a fixed path of discovery and delivery (Figure 2-1). In this model, the library is situated at the end of the chain, which suggests that the role of the library in collecting, and therefore providing, information is consumer-based. It belies the library's necessarily complex role as a broker of scholarly communication and catalyst in the research process.

The library's traditional internal supply chain can be represented as a similar static model resembling a chain (Figure 2-2). Acquisitions ends up between the selection and access functions, seemingly linking the two via a third, nebulous function of "getting" things. This static model represents an acquisitions function based on procurement, the singular act of *buying.* Significantly, this internal supply chain does not typically factor

Statement on Principles and Standards of Acquisitions Practice

In all acquisitions transactions, a librarian:

1. gives first consideration to the objectives and policies of his or her institution;

2. strives to obtain the maximum ultimate value of each dollar of expenditure;

3. grants all competing vendors equal consideration insofar as the established policies of his or her library permit, and regards each transaction on its own merits;

4. subscribes to and works for honesty, truth, and fairness in buying and selling, and denounces all forms and manifestations of bribery;

5. declines personal gifts and gratuities;

6. uses only by consent original ideas and designs devised by one vendor for competitive purchasing purposes;

7. accords a prompt and courteous reception insofar as conditions permit to all who call on legitimate business missions;

8. fosters and promotes fair, ethical, and legal trade practices;

9. avoids sharp practice;

10. strives consistently for knowledge of the publishing and bookselling industry;

11. strives to establish practical and efficient methods for the conduct of his/her office;

12. counsels and assists fellow acquisitions librarians in the performance of their duties, whenever occasion permits.

Developed by the ALCTS (Association for Library Collections and Technical Services) Acquisitions Section Ethics Task Force; endorsed by the ALCTS Acquisitions Section; and adopted by the ALCTS Board of Directors, Midwinter Meeting, February 7, 1994. (ALCTS, 1994)

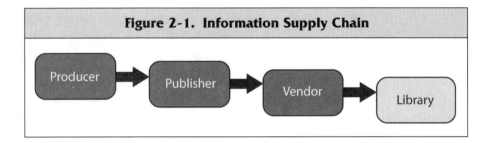

Figure 2-1. Information Supply Chain

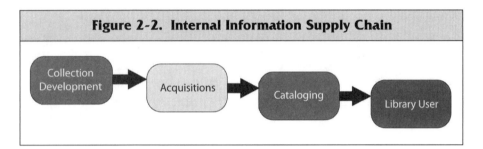

Figure 2-2. Internal Information Supply Chain

in the complex kinds of problem solving that any practitioner of contemporary acquisitions faces when expanding the library's sphere of access.

These models, which fix both acquisitions and the library in a static position in their respective information supply chains, are no longer as relevant as they were before the information age. In the first model above, the library is positioned as an end point for the process of information dissemination, a sort of warehouse that information eventually trickles down to. This implies a passive role in the information universe. In the second model, acquisitions functions merely as an intermediary, positioned to *react* to order requests from collection development and then *react* again to receipts from the supplier. These chains are part of a semantic geography of information based on a *process of moving*; they are fixed paths for transporting physical items. The rigidity of such models is well suited to an older paradigm of information distribution, discovery, and access where linear movement of information could be safely assumed. However, the nonlinearity of electronic resources is well established (Burnette 2008), and this breakdown of traditional lines of acquisition has come to engulf all possible formats (see Chapter 3).

In these models, acquisitions ends up situated between two intellectual processes. The first process involves the production of scholarly communication, where information is published as content. The second process is dissemination, of which collection building is a part. Scholarly communication is selected and made accessible vis-à-vis the mission and service goals of the library, which builds up a collection that will hopefully be of use to the community it supports. Acquisitions ends up having a kind of mediating role where its primary function is to bridge two processes, one where content is identified and selected, and another where that content is made available to library users through a number of channels.

When the supply of and demand for information were achieved through a model that assumed the primacy of paper, the notion of the supply chain and the accompanying, fixed channels of communication were fairly easy to understand. In all cases, there was something physical that had to be acted upon, something tangible: information could be shipped, stamped, shelved, and circulated (or not). To create efficiency in a process of moving things from multiple publishers to multiple libraries, the rise of third-party vendors (also "jobbers" in the book trade and "agents" in the serials business) was natural. The vendors became a single service point for libraries to work with and, in basic terms, continue to provide the same kinds of services at the present time for physical-format media. Jobbers, for example, allow for shipping, invoicing, and claiming from a single service point. Serials agents function slightly differently, handling renewals, invoicing, and claiming but not usually handling the actual physical issues in a subscription. The mediating role of vendors in terms of physical items is critical: by centralizing the functions associated with distribution, leveraging high-volume ordering per publisher to maximize discounts, and consolidating the service points for all publishers and libraries with whom the vendor does business, a maximum efficiency, and therefore savings, can be achieved.

Once establishing a partnership with a vendor, the role of acquisitions becomes slightly more complicated. Vendors simplify the procurement of material in many ways, but they also add value in many other ways as a service provider. When working with the vendor, these available services become another mechanism through which content acquisition can be actively managed. In addition to supplying materials, the vendor also can consolidate information that directly relates to the library's construction of its sphere of access. Services might include the supply of prepublication data from multiple vendors, provision of content in a variety of media, and discounts for volume purchasing. Often a vendor will provide this value-added information in real time through their online Web interface, especially "e-slips" (see the following section, "Vendors and Vendoring").

When it was limited to physical items that were created through a means of mechanical production (or reproduction) and physical distribution, the role of acquisitions was secured in a fixed chain that mediated *selection of* and *access to* content. In a sense, acquisitions practitioners were almost entirely concerned with getting a *container* (e.g., a book) into the building— with the building itself functioning as a sort of metacontainer. This resulted in a linear model of collection building that was unidirectional and inflexible (Figure 2-3). However, when not completely tied to physical-format items, the linearity of the process breaks down. In collections that include intangible media, such as e-books or streaming videos, the entire approach must change (see Chapter 3).

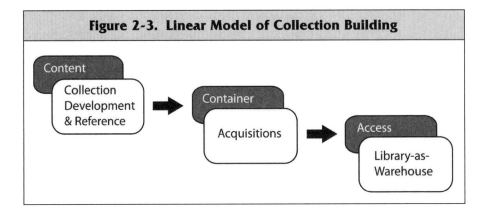

Vendors and "Vendoring"

Vendors are strategic partners in creating the sphere of access through which the library connects to content of increasing amount and variety. While their role in the emerging electronic information marketplace was once uncertain, the value that vendors add is now more important than ever. With the explosion of available and therefore potentially discoverable information, the library must continue to find ways to work through strategic partnerships to keep up with changes in production of and demand for various kinds of information.

Vendors tend to be thought of in terms of discounting items. That is part of the calculus used when selecting a vendor, consistent with the second principle of acquisitions practice, which affirms that an acquisitions librarian "strives to obtain the maximum ultimate value of each dollar of expenditure" (ALCTS, 1994). But while the discount is important when considering the library's budget, unit price is, in the end, only part of the calculus. The part of acquisitions that is a business does require a business strategy, and that part of the strategy inevitably focuses on financial considerations. More is at stake when considering the role of the vendor for content provision, however. While acquisitions is partly about managing business transactions and relationships, it also includes customer service, technical processing, and product support, too. Managing the incoming content in a timely manner (regardless of format), updating the online records, and processing materials for return constitute just a few areas of concern for an acquisitions practitioner that might be aided by vendor services. Working with a vendor to develop shelf-ready processing for items, record downloads for purchased materials, and a protocol for handling the return of items—either duplicated or damaged—is a critical element in the partnership that acquisitions must forge with library vendors. By emphasizing the role of the vendor as an overall *strategic* partner rather than just a business partner, a given acquisitions operation is likely to achieve a great deal more than if the vendor is considered only in terms of the bottom line. Therefore, while considering the potential savings, the cost alone should not drive all acquisitions decisions. The second principle should be applied only in conjunction with the first, which "gives first consideration to the objectives and policies of his or

Selecting a Vendor

Methods for selecting a vendor may include the following:

- Formal request for proposal (RFP)
- Professional references
- Vendor visit to campus
- Librarian, staff, and/or administrator visit to vendor site
- Conference presentation
- Mandate from a procurement or administrative office

Some considerations when making a vendor selection:

- Pricing of content (including discount structure and any service fees)
- Shipping (costs, packing options, scheduling)
- Web-based account management system
- Physical processing (if applicable) and associated costs
- E-content licensing and registration (if applicable)
- Approval plan
- Return and cancellation policy (including credits)
- Invoicing format and payment terms
- Level of customer service

her institution" (ALCTS, 1994). While financial considerations will be a part of an institution's objectives and policies, ultimately service will play a key role as well. Discussing the library's strategy with vendors and understanding, in turn, each vendor's available services and service limitations will allow acquisitions to support library end users according to the library's mission.

Developing a significant role for a vendor and, ultimately, the group of vendors within the practice of acquisitions must start before the vendor is selected. Acquisitions, in conjunction with the rest of the library, must be able to clearly articulate not only the financial requirements needed to meet their goals but also any value-added services that a vendor must supply for the library to meet that end. Such services might include those outsourced from the library, such as **physical processing** of print books, including full preparation of **shelf-ready** materials, or the negotiation of boilerplate license terms for e-resources. But such services might also include customization of the interface to the **online vendor database** or the format that the invoices are delivered in. Most vendors are fairly flexible in terms of what services they can provide and what options are available within those services. Frequently it comes down to how valuable the service is to the library and how much, therefore, the library is willing and able to pay.

When searching for a vendor, particularly a principal vendor or one that the library will be doing

---

Definition: **physical processing**

Preparing an item for library use. Such processing might include any combination of bar coding, property stamping, adding security devices, bookplating, covering, or binding. Many vendors offer services where they will process items on behalf of the library for a fee, often as part of an **approval plan** (see definition in the following section).

Definition: **shelf-ready**

Items that are completely physically processed by a vendor to be ready for shelving as soon as the items are checked in at the library.

a large volume of business with, all of the financial and service requirements should be carefully detailed in the **request for proposal (RFP)**. Whether being opened to all potential vendors or only sent to select prescreened vendors, the RFP will outline and contextualize the library's needs in a formal document. Any interested vendors will respond with their proposal, detailing the services they can provide, associated costs, and any other terms, conditions, or additional services that may be applied. Though typically the library has some latitude in drafting and negotiating an RFP, the document may be subject to regulations set by the library administration, college or university procurement policies, or even state law. Libraries involved with one or more consortium may need to take preexisting commitments into account when creating and negotiating the RFP.

It is important to note that the RFP process is a serious one, and should be treated as such at all times. Besides showing

Definition: **online vendor database**

A book vendor's or subscription agent's Web-based inventory and ordering system. The most advanced of these systems allow for online ordering, real-time ordering, inventory status, integration with the library's approval plan, and other enhanced features. Examples of online vendor databases include:

- Blackwell's Collection Manager
- Coutts's OASIS
- EBSCO's EBSCONET
- Harrassowitz's OttoEditions and OttoSerials
- Swets's SwetsWise
- YBP's GOBI

Definition: **request for proposal (RFP)**

A process by which the library requests bids from vendors as part of a formal selection process. Besides volume and price of items, the RFP usually indicates other service requirements, such as shipping costs, processing specifications, and anything else related to the provision of content to the library. The successful bid is awarded a contract for the services requested.

Selecting a Vendor

Choosing a vendor and developing a working relationship with that vendor is a critical part of acquisitions. The partnership with each vendor that the library uses is an important link in the chain between content production and content consumption by library users. While vendors are businesses that are trying to make money, the value they add to content acquisitions likely far exceeds what their services cost each library. Vendors usually offer many services. At their most basic, they provide a single point for order submissions and any subsequent claims, consolidated invoicing for content and any associated services, and regular delivery of content. Additionally, vendors might provide additional services such as processing of physical-format items, provision of bibliographic records for acquired content, and out-of-print searching.

Because the ability of the vendor to provide content and related services has such an impact on the library, vendor decisions should be carefully considered. In some cases, either the vendor or a university (or both) might require a signed contract in place before the vendor begins supplying content or services for which the library will be billed. This might be standard practice or only apply to a certain volume of business or type of service. When in doubt, checking with the library administration or campus procurement office may be a good first step. Often, a contract will be preceded by a formal RFP process where vendors interested in doing business with the library may be thoroughly evaluated. However, it is unlikely that an RFP will be required for every acquisition situation.

(Continued on facing page)

professional courtesy and respect to those vendors who are competing for the library's business, the acquisitions practitioner has an opportunity to review detailed and potentially sensitive information about each of the bidding vendors. Handling of such details is codified in the "Statement on Principles and Standards of Acquisitions Practice" (see earlier sidebar), requiring

Selecting a Vendor *(Continued)*

Whether or not a vendor is being reviewed through a formal competitive process, several factors should be considered before selecting a vendor for content supply. Some questions to keep in mind are:

- What is it that I am trying to acquire? Does this vendor specialize in this kind of content?
- What value will this vendor add to the acquisitions process (e.g., savings in time, significant discounting, quality customer support, etc.)?
- Are there other vendors that specialize in providing this particular content and/or service?
- Does this vendor deal only or primarily with the library community?
- What experiences have my colleagues had with this vendor? Do my colleagues have experience with other vendors providing this same function or set of functions?
- What are my expectations for content delivery? For invoicing? For customer service? Have I communicated these expectations to the vendor and received adequate assurance that my expectations will be met?

When working with a vendor, it is better to discuss expectations, establish service benchmarks, and ask questions up front. While a formal RFP may specify many of the performance and cost requirements, any business relationship should be based on a mutual understanding of the library's content and service needs, on the one hand, and the vendor's ability to meet those needs on the other.

that the acquisitions professional "grants all competing vendors equal consideration insofar as the established policies of his or her library permit, and regards each transaction on its own merits" (ALCTS, 1994, Statement 3). Additionally, as the RFP may contain highly specific offers, it is also essential to keep in mind that an acquisitions professional is bound to obtain consent prior to using "original ideas and designs devised by one vendor for competitive purchasing purposes" (ALCTS, 1994, Statement 6). In circumstances where local policy requires an RFP or multiple bids prior to retaining a vendor but a given product or service can only be provided by a single vendor, extra documentation is generally required in advance of a commitment being formalized.

RFPs can be time-consuming and even tedious to draft but represent a key tool for developing an effective plan, in terms of both content and budget. The important thing to keep in mind is that RFPs are useful only when identical or interchangeable items and services can be supplied from multiple vendors. This makes RFPs especially useful in the print-based world, where vendors can supply, for example, the same book or journal. However, where a product or service is uniquely offered from a single vendor—in the case of many databases or publisher-specific packages, for example—a route of direct negotiation must be taken. Negotiations provide the library some potential for lowering price, customizing access, or allowing some technical manipulation of the product. Negotiation, however, does not represent a free-for-all. While an acquisitions professional should give "first consideration to the objectives and policies of his or her institution" (ALCTS, 1994, Statement 1), it is critical that one "avoids **sharp practice**" (ALCTS, 1994, Statement 9) in working with sellers in any context. Whether working with a vendor through an RFP, a publisher during a license negotiation, or a customer service representative over a single book, professional and personal ethics matter. As a matter of course, it is expected that an acquisitions professional "fosters and promotes fair, ethical, and legal trade practices" (ALCTS, 1994, Statement 8).

Definition: **sharp practice**

Gaining an advantage using unfair or dishonest methods.

Microcosm: The Approval Plan

The **approval plan** was developed as a method of bringing materials into the library's sphere of access with a minimal amount of effort on the part of both the library and the book vendor. Through the approval plan, which today can function with a high degree of nuance and customization, content is identified and delivered to the library automatically. With library-provided selection criteria, including subject (e.g., Library of Congress classification) and nonsubject criteria (e.g., publisher), material can easily be identified and provided by the vendor, maximizing the efficiency of the collection-building process.

Definition: **approval plan**

A vendor service where new title notifications or books are supplied automatically according to a profile developed in conjunction with the library. Many approval plans include other optional services, such as enhanced catalog records for approval content, shelf-ready materials, or e-book provision, which are likewise part of the library's content **profile**.

Subject criteria are often based on either the Library of Congress or Dewey classification schemes. Those criteria considered "nonsubject" include categories such as publisher, series, or price limits. This allows maximum flexibility in designing a selection mechanism based on any number of pertinent factors as determined by the library. Many plans are sophisticated to the degree that as long as the library is able to provide a selection rule, the criteria can be used in defining the sphere of access made available by the vendor. Approval plans are offered by most major domestic and foreign vendors; configurations of the respective plans are specific to each vendor. It should be kept in mind that these plans, the instruments used to set them up, and the systems used to administer them are typically proprietary, incorporating "original ideas and designs devised by one vendor for competitive purchasing purposes" (ALCTS,

1994, Statement 6). Specifics from one vendor's plan should not be shared with another vendor.

At its core, the approval plan represents a kind of blurring of boundaries between collection development and acquisitions, as the plan automates several aspects of each respective function. As approval plans become more sophisticated, they likewise become more nuanced even as they become more totalizing; in other words, approval plans provide a means of applying increasingly granular selection rules to an increasingly large body of content. Despite the approval plan's fundamental grounding in the selection of content, management of the plan almost inevitably impacts acquisitions: ordering, shipping, invoicing, and returns all dovetail with the functioning of the plan. Therefore, it may make sense for the administration of the plan, typically via the vendor's online database, to be the responsibility of acquisitions. No matter who in the library is responsible for the maintenance of the library's plan, acquisitions must work closely with collection development in addition to the vendor.

A well-developed approval plan can draw a significant amount of content into the library's sphere. At its most basic level, the plan will provide an advanced notification system, either through the automatic supply of paper slips or, more frequently now, the provision of electronic title notification via e-slips according to the **profile**. While many libraries have been reluctant to give up paper slips, there are undeniable advantages to the use of electronic slips. Since the slips are really representative

Definition: **profile**

The often elaborate criteria by which the vendor supplies content to the library on an automatic basis via the approval plan. The process of determining these criteria is an ongoing dialectic between the library and vendor that improves the accuracy and efficiency of the approval plan over time. The initial setup of a profile is called "profiling."

of the information in the vendor's database, e-slips can provide real-time updates on title availability, price, order status, and if the title was already acquired by the library. A vendor may also be able to load the library's holdings directly into their database, making that tool even more comprehensive. E-slips can also provide a strategic advantage in providing live links to reviews, tables of contents, and book jackets. Other advanced features may be available through e-slips, including subject and author information, links to other titles in a series, and shared information among other customers of that vendor. In some advanced systems, vendors may actually allow previews of e-book content, linked directly from the e-slip. In all, e-slips provide unprecedented access to content during the decision-making process.

With the highly flexible nature of most contemporary approval plans and numerous integrated service options available from vendors, libraries are able to partner with one or more vendors to create an expandable and customizable sphere of access. Those plans that capitalize on the online environment provide opportunities for discovery coupled with significant resources to aid in decision making. The Web-based vendor databases allow for streamlined selection, efficient ordering, and granular reporting, including some financial data. Since such nuanced and comprehensive systems encourage the consolidation of acquisitions functions, it is imperative that any vendor is carefully evaluated prior to establishing a business relationship. This can be achieved most successfully through a well-structured RFP that elicits a detailed response and encourages conversation. Discussion with colleagues, attendance at related conference sessions, and regular evaluation of the vendor can help ensure that quality is maintained on a continuous basis.

The result of developing an approval plan is a sophisticated tool for filtering and managing the ever-expanding information universe while supporting a likewise ever-expanding array of library

Approval Plans

Approval plans represent a sophisticated, customizable tool that can be used to achieve the library's selection and acquisition goals with a minimum of effort and a maximum of efficiency. When implementing a new plan, modifying an existing plan, or changing approval vendors, the outcome of an approval plan depends on all stakeholders clearly articulating their goals for the plan at the outset and working collaboratively—both before and after the plan is in place—in order to develop and refine the plan over time.

Example 1: Research Library

In the case of a large research library, the overall collection focus is likely to be on specialized collections carefully curated to meet the long-term needs of the research community. At the same time, the library will also support a large population of students and faculty who have need for a broad collection of general content for their studies and teaching. In this environment, it is not possible to pick general, mainstream titles individually. For the broad, basic coverage required by a large academic population, a book plan can automate what would otherwise be a rote and time-consuming process through the selection and acquisition cycle. Besides having books selected and delivered automatically through an approval plan, the physical items can be processed by the vendor and come shelf-ready with customized physical processing, which might include bar codes, slip pockets, property stamps, radio-frequency identification (RFID) tags, call number labels, or security strips. Other processing options may be available, as well, though the amount of physical processing could significantly impact the per-item price.

This level of automation allows the selectors to focus on their research areas, finding specialized content and investigating resources specific to their collections.

Example 2: Liberal Arts College

Unlike a research university, the content acquired in a liberal arts college library is focused on providing a wide variety of content for a

(Continued)

Approval Plans (Continued)

primarily undergraduate population. Besides the difference in the size and needs of the library users, resources—including money, space, and personnel—are generally more limited than they are in a research environment. The library's content is more likely to support curricular needs rather than high-level research.

In this circumstance, the approval plan can be used in different ways than in a research library. One strategy might be to have most of the library's monographic content delivered on approval. Instead of relying on a book plan to fill in just the core of the collection, the process of building much of the collection can be mostly automated. This would relieve the librarians of almost all title-level collection decisions in order to focus on instruction and assisting students with individual research needs. Or the library could set up a slip-only plan. This would give the selectors more control over the budget, which can be critical in situations where the budget is small or funding is unstable. This option requires title-by-title decisions, though for a relatively small number of overall selections.

Because approval plans are adaptable, they can be customized to fit any situation. However, because of the freedom in creating and administering an approval plan, it is important to always think about the library's mission and available resources when developing such a plan.

Blanket Plans

Similar to approval plans are blanket plans. In these plans, libraries agree to accept and pay for all the content shipped by a vendor from a specific publisher or region. If effectively managed by both the vendor and the library, this can be a way to obtain difficult-to-find materials. Because the material provided on such a plan is both uncertain and nonreturnable, such a plan is best set up in support of a research collection.

user needs and expectations. In addition to identifying mainstream publications from major publishers, a well-honed approval plan also has the potential to help bring **gray literature** into the library's sphere. Also called "fugitive literature" (Chapman, 2004: 30), this broad category of information includes many types of publications—including reports of all kinds, conference proceedings, technical papers, and other content that may be marginal in terms of established distribution channels. Besides limited distribution, a lack of indexing or other bibliographic control may also increase the difficulty of discovery (Plutchak, 2007). However, while difficult to identify, such content may nonetheless be essential to meeting user needs. Even when gray literature is covered by an approval plan, it is likely that some of this content will fall outside the approval profile and will need to be sought out directly by acquisitions, either through specialized vendors or even an open Web search. Additionally, gray literature might also fall into one of the categories of "free" content, discussed in Chapter 3, and therefore not qualify for inclusion in an approval plan.

Definition: **gray literature**

Content produced and distributed outside mainstream publication channels. Such content will likely be most important to research or technical libraries.

The Access Imperative in Acquisitions

The ultimate role of acquisitions should most properly be associated with *access to* content rather than the *purchase of* materials. It is true that there is more to librarianship than providing access, and that other service areas of the library contribute to providing access to library users. However, libraries exist primarily to bring a set of *information*, qua *content*, together in such a way as to make that content available when needed. Access is a mission-driven function and a localized practice. Even the idea of what constitutes "access" becomes a context-specific concept. A library supporting a small liberal arts college may be most concerned with providing a breadth of content that is readily accessible. A library at a research university may be more focused on the future access of information, especially in particular subject areas, which results in an *anticipated* rather than *acute* information need. In both the preceding cases, there are likely special collections that are unique and serve one or many different functions beyond the scope of the general collection. The changing information universe does not undermine the need for unique content, locally focused collections, or long-term preservation as demanded by a given situation. However, changes in content production and consumption complicate both the mission and the practice of every library in terms of both access and preservation.

Access has become increasingly detached from ownership in many, though certainly not all, cases. This means that acquisitions may not always—or may not even mostly—be dealing with straightforward purchasing of content. However, the proliferation of formats has also changed the nature of ownership. While ownership undoubtedly remains a requirement for certain kinds of content, the dichotomy of owning or not owning is no longer the entirely meaningful principle that it was just a few years ago. Lee (2000) has postulated moving away from such a dichotomy because of differences in the perceived meaning of the idea of *ownership* between information professionals and information users. While the latter focus on "access and convenience," the former "are mostly concerned with how to secure and control information resources as well as the legal ramifications of doing so" (Lee, 2000: 1108). The question of defining and managing ownership has become only more complicated as the information age matures. The result is an "ownership continuum," where the rights to access, archive, distribute, and so on for a particular content object can be thought of in terms of degrees instead of absolutes (Figure 2-4). This shift to a more nuanced approach to access rights has changed in much the same way as the now-superseded dichotomy of print or electronic, which is discussed in detail in Chapter 3.

Regardless of where on the continuum of ownership the library's access rights fall, the library will likely have to pay for those rights, whether access is through ownership, site license, or pay-per-view. This will include directly tracking the library's budget allocation(s) for content acquisition while staying aware of external economic conditions. Variables such as global financial crises, university budget projections, and currency exchange rates should be accounted for when monitoring the library's own funding. To maintain access, whether in the form of regularly scheduled book shipments or uninterrupted database searching, invoices should be paid promptly. Discrepancies between expected content and delivered content, which will inevitably arise, need to be brought to the vendor's attention immediately. Situations will vary and it should not automatically be assumed that withholding the library's payment to a given vendor is the most appropriate way of dealing with

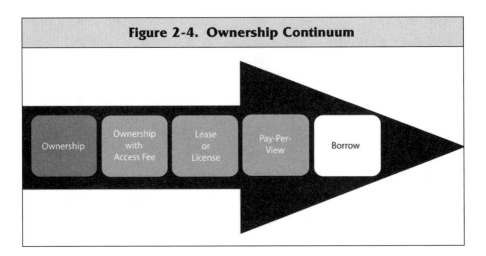

Figure 2-4. Ownership Continuum

Ownership | Ownership with Access Fee | Lease or License | Pay-Per-View | Borrow

Ownership Considerations

In a print collection, ownership and perpetual access are implied in the acquisition (i.e., purchase) of content, even if that perpetual access is not guaranteed (e.g., items can be stolen, destroyed, etc.). With the ascendance of e-resources, perpetual access must be explicitly provided by the publisher and often must be specifically negotiated for by the library. The access requirements in any given acquisitions situation are likely to be variable and contingent on several factors, such as the library's mission, the materials budget, and even the specific resource being acquired.

1. **The mission:** Who is using the collection? Is library content supporting a general curriculum, an interdisciplinary project, or a comprehensive research collection? The resources being acquired will need to be managed in light of their intended or probable use starting at the beginning of the acquisitions process to ensure that those resources support the end users for whom the content is being acquired.

2. **The resources:** In the end, it may not be necessary—or even desirable—to own all resources that the library users want to access, even if the library is in the enviable position of being able to buy all selected content. For many continuing e-resources, it may be better in the long run to lease or subscribe to content. If content is updated regularly, paying an annual or per-access fee might be more cost effective and prove easier to manage in the long run than a collection that has to be actively managed by library professionals.

3. **The budget:** Options for access may, in the end, depend on the budget despite all other considerations. While perpetual access might be a stated ideal of a particular acquisitions program, it simply may not be possible. As budgets continue to tighten, a strategic balance between owning a limited amount content in perpetuity and accessing a broader range of user-requested content in a timely manner will become more important even as it becomes more difficult to manage.

problems or misunderstandings. Possible remedies may include returning wrong or damaged materials, crossing a line item off the invoice prior to payment, or the issuing of a credit memo by the vendor to indicate that a payment has been credited to the library's account.

Many libraries do not directly pay vendors for content but rather have payment issued through a central payments office on campus. While more efficient and secure for the university, such a process often results in a lag between the processing of an invoice in acquisitions and payment being issued to vendors by the university. Most library vendors are set up to accommodate the delay. Several options may be considered for expediting payments when necessary, though all such options are subject to local contingencies and regulations. One option is connecting the acquisitions module of the ILS directly to the university accounting system to process payments directly in the library system. While this can be a very effective means of getting payments processed and issued to vendors, the technical barriers to such an interface can be substantial. Acquisitions can also configure **electronic data interchange (EDI)** with vendors to receive electronic invoices directly in the ILS. Again, such an exchange is dependent on the technical ability of both the library and the vendor(s) to implement such a process with their respective systems. One of the most effective means for issuing payment to a supplier is the use of an institutional credit or purchasing card, often referred to as a "**p-card**." While

---

Definition: **electronic data interchange (EDI)**

A protocol for the electronic transmission of information. Libraries may be able to set up EDI for ordering, invoicing, or even claiming missing content from vendors through the ILS. Two common EDI standards used within the library environment are EDIFACT and X12.

Definition: **p-card**

A credit card issued by the university for university-related purchasing.

---

the p-card allows for instantaneous payment, someone will be required to keep the appropriate records for purchases made with the p-card and balance the monthly statement. Such responsibility usually resides in acquisitions. Like any credit card, purchases may carry some risk, either because the Web connection is not encrypted or the account information is not kept secure by the seller. When a p-card is issued to acquisitions, it is important to keep the account information secure in the library and watch the statements carefully to ensure that the account has not been compromised when making purchases throughout the month.

Sphere of Access

Instead of operating (solely) within an aggregated collection of physical items where access is achieved through a number of labor-intensive, if ingenious, mechanical access apparatuses, the library community must now be concerned with its *sphere of access*. This would be all information available to the library community, whether or not it is owned by or contained in the library. This partial dissolution of the library as an entirely, or principally, physical collection necessarily includes access points well beyond the scope of acquisitions, such as one library community's access to other libraries' resources—or even the open Internet (e.g., Google, etc.). However, the implications of this dissolution of the "library as building" for the structure and practice of acquisitions remains profound. In essence, the contemporary library collection is expandable in infinite directions; in theory, today's library collection may even be considered infinitely expandable. It seems that the limits on potentially available information recede further into the distance with each passing day. Exceptions do, and will continue to, exist in the trends that drive the dissolution of the library as warehouse. Such notable exceptions include rare, local, and ephemeral materials. However, even in these cases—the rare books and the archives—the ability to produce digital simulacra of these objects is dissolving even this final frontier of physicality. Not that the originals can be entirely ignored or replaced, but that in many cases access to the copy of an item serves much the same purpose as access to the original. The exceptions to this stream-lined access by way of proxy will continue to be a diminishing point on the access horizon.

Today, we must be more consistent about speaking in terms of *spheres* rather than *collections*. This is not to diminish the role of the collection in meeting information needs, but instead to turn the traditional approach to access on its proverbial head. Rather than taking the collection to be the primary mode of access, it is, instead, part of the makeup of that total sphere of access. This represents a major realignment of content within the information universe. Content comes now in many formats (see Chapter 3), and the format of choice, where there is one, will depend on need and preferred mode of access. Use of con-tent is now more user driven, and therefore acquisitions must necessarily become at once more flexible as it becomes more complex. Acquisitions must also engage with the collection-building process in a more collaborative way, working closely not just with publishers and content vendors but with other service units within the library. Such engagement follows Pritchard's deconstructed definition of the library, where the library is framed in terms of a "suite of services designed to meet a range of needs" rather than "a single definition of a collection in a building, designed to work in one, linear way" (Pritchard, 2008: 222). This flexible and collaborative ap-proach requires a kind of processual nimbleness coupled with an expertise on available content sources in order to respond as rapidly as possible. Increasingly, acquisitions may even be work-ing with the library users themselves in an expanded capacity. Some examples of content realignment within the information universe that have directly impacted contemporary acquisitions include digitization of **local content** or other **rare content**, the expansion of **consortia** and other alliance-based information access, and the **open access** movement.

Within the library itself, the licensing of materials has created various possibilities and degrees of access that are far more context and content specific than ever before. Sometimes licensed access is tied to print, though often it is not. What becomes critical in this complex world of information interaction is clearly identifying what the library community needs to access and knowing (or correctly anticipating) what uses the content will be subject to once access is achieved by a user. A priority has also arisen for acquisitions, like the rest of the library, to meet content needs in real time. Acquisitions practitioners must be prepared to facilitate access to content whether it is in a traditional form or not.

Acquisitions practice, like all genres of library work, has been changed by the growing volume, acceptance, and usage

Definition: **local content**

Content that has been produced locally and may have limited distribution or relevance. A newsletter from a local historical society or video of a town hall meeting are examples of local content.

Definition: **rare content**

Content that is difficult to access. Though the paragon of rare library materials is the rare book, rare content might also include sites from the "hidden" Web or electronic content contained in an obsolete format. Rare content is often more challenging to obtain than other content and may have contingencies regarding access or long-term preservation. Content stored in an obsolete format, such as BetaMax tapes or floppy discs, may require likewise obsolete hardware to access the content.

Definition: **consortium [*pl.* consortia]**

A group of organizations that work together as a single entity. For purchasing, a consortium is the mechanism by which many libraries come together in order to leverage their buying power when acquiring (especially electronic) content.

Definition: **open access (OA)**

At its most basic, the OA movement is about removing barriers to information access by making research available free online. Advocates for OA are found among librarians, researchers, legislators, and publishers. A major objective is to make content, especially journal articles based on publicly funded research, as widely available and easily accessible as possible. This is in part a reaction to increases in serial pricing, diminishing library budgets, economic inequality, and other barriers to access.

of electronic-based media, any content that is enscripted and disseminated throughout the information universe in an electronic format. Acquisitions has largely become a reactive practice over time, one where practitioners struggle to keep up with a proliferation of resources, agreements, and content management technologies by absorbing new kinds of content and practice into existing processes and workflows. This reactive practice has, to various degrees, marginalized the practice of acquisitions within the library. While the world dominated by the physical item made acquisitions as much about *getting things* as *obtaining access* (the two practices were often the same, or at least simultaneous), navigation of information sources and formats has grown increasingly complex. No longer is acquisitions merely a set of clerical practices that functions merely to type and mail orders and then to check receipts and pay invoices. Redundancy, propriety, nontraditional use, and proliferation of access points have all combined, with other challenges, to change the way acquisitions is done, and therefore the way that acquisitions should be thought about. Confusion, frustration, and inefficiency occur when the new imperatives to create a sphere of access are imposed on a clerical model centered on physical items. Acquisitions must play a role that emphasizes the strategic, legitimate, and ethical appropriation of content over the mechanical process whereby items are procured.

Strategic Thinking about Access

While the dominant ideas for strategic acquisition of content in a paradigm of print resources relied almost entirely on cost-cutting solutions for physical items—shipping, processing, receiving—these are just some of the elements that must be considered in contemporary acquisitions. And while tangible material will clearly play some role in most collections indefinitely, the time and energy available for this kind of content is increasingly marginalized. Experience with e-journals, for example, has definitively proven diminishing returns vis-à-vis all inputs—time, energy, and money—for traditional print-based journal processing in libraries in cases where electronic access is available for general research needs. What is presented to the acquisitions practitioner today is a vast array of potential sources and possibilities for content production and dissemination. To meet the requirements of complex collection development and the increasingly sophisticated demands of library users, the acquisitions practitioner must be prepared to bring a nuanced strategic approach to both sourcing and providing access to required content.

This validates neither the proverbial "end of print" long feared in scholarly communication nor the similarly extreme assertion that "format does not matter." These two misguided clichés were born with the World Wide Web and have proven to be quite pervasive concerns in terms of both scholarly and professional culture. The expectation seems to be that either all information will be electronic (produced in or converted to an electronic-based format) or that so much information will be digitized that it will not matter if something happens to exist in print as long as it can be accessed. The fact is that in some ways, print actually matters *more* than it ever has before. Manhoff (2006) makes the compelling case that limitations inherent to the production and distribution of information objects in

Alternate Modes of Acquisition

Content realignments often pose various challenges to acquisitions, especially any practice based in a traditional paradigm.

   Local and rare content may not be available through vendors and may involve additional units of the library, such as special collections or even the director's office. Acquisition of local or rare content may involve cultivating local contacts that are not traditional vendors, and taking possession of material may involve actually picking material up in person. Local content may include content produced by campus departments, municipal historical societies, or regional auction houses, among many other possible sources not likely to be handled by a commercial vendor. Rare materials might come from such different sources as specialized dealers or online auctions; the complexities in cases of rare materials come not only from rareness (the difficulty to find due to age, limited production, or both), but also from the unique properties of the rare object—the inherent worth of the content-as-object. In both of these cases—local and rare material—archival considerations are likely to be of major concern, as well (see Chapter 3).

   Working with a consortium (or several consortia) often provides opportunities for deep discounting and centralized licensing, which can be a significant benefit to libraries. The opportunity for the vendor or publisher to sell to multiple sites in a single deal can be a major incentive to the seller, as well. However, working with a consortium adds an administrative layer for individual libraries that sometimes results in additional work for acquisitions, whether or not the library is working with a vendor or serial agent in addition to the consortium for

(Continued on facing page)

specific formats, including both print and electronic, means these objects, even when the *information* itself is identical, cannot be treated as *identical* objects. Electronic formats will have their own distinct features and limitations, as will their print counterparts—if such counterparts exist. While acquisitions has always responded to the decision making of collection

Alternate Modes of Acquisition *(Continued)*

the purposes of invoicing and access. For example, if a consortium has negotiated a significant discount on a major journal package but has problems billing efficiently, it may be in a library's best interest to subscribe through their preferred subscription agent. Conversely, even if an agent provides timely invoicing and a well-organized online subscription management interface, such services may not be enough to turn down the deep discounting achieved by a consortium. In any case, consortial opportunities and obligations can be a major strategic consideration in sourcing content, particularly resources that have a recurring annual cost.

Open access (OA) is a growing movement to make critical research, especially government or other publicly funded research, available online free of charge. Momentum for the movement has been fueled by the perception of unfair pricing of research journals by commercial publishers. When high-profile journals are made available freely online, such as the *Public Library of Science (PLoS)* (http://www .plos.org), it is sometimes difficult to determine whether the resource is being acquired or if it is functionally just another free Internet resource. With no tangible piece to obtain and no invoice to pay, the access can be determined and periodically checked by the collection development department; access can be provided through the Integrated Library System by cataloging. Acquisitions may act on an OA title, however, if the journal is added to some content management system, such as a link resolver. Given the ongoing questions concerning the stability of OA publishing, it may be some time before this category of publication can be adequately addressed in a model for acquisitions.

development by finding an item that contains the content being sought, there is an emerging role for acquisitions to help identify the *specific* format once the content decision has been made by collection development. This implies an interaction both within the library and with the selected content beyond the traditional role of acquisitions. By extension, acquisitions needs to be included in the larger intellectual and service mission of the library.

For libraries to succeed, it is critical that those who are organizing and practicing acquisitions take a proactive, forward-thinking role in developing techniques that are general and adaptable enough that they can account for many formats without necessarily assuming one to be dominant. Though it may be possible and perhaps necessary to establish and maintain several subprocesses within acquisitions (Burnette, 2008), a context-specific approach that is goal oriented rather than process oriented may be most appropriate. While utilizing routines where necessary, an approach focused on access outcomes will be more likely to absorb the constant irregularities of content acquisitions.

Conclusion: Information (Re)alignment

Acquisitions is responsible for the same basic functional categories that it always has been and operates within the same basic ethical framework. At the same time, significant changes in both the library and larger information environments have fundamentally altered what it means to *do acquisitions*. The move away from static supply chains of scholarly information within a larger context of information realignment has resulted in a nuanced matrix of information production and consumption. Within this (re)alignment, the central function of acquisitions as the locus of a strategy-based information practice has not changed but shifted to be one that demands a more proactive practice. User preference in both searching and accessing information has demonstrated a clear "shift of interest to the piece rather than the container, the article rather than the journal, the definition rather than the dictionary" (Van Orsdel, 2007: 204). The disaggregation of units of information from composite wholes extends beyond journals and databases to both reference resources and even general academic texts, as e-book platforms allow both full-text searches of monographic content and subsequent results ranking by chapter (see Chapter 3 for more about e-books). The increasingly granular specificity of information sought by library users has significant implications for acquisitions, as changes in user demands will drive changes in the resources that are acquired.

The key to adapting in this new paradigm "is in reorienting our work to a much more refined definition of services, focusing on unique strengths, local needs, and multiple ways of delivering information" (Pritchard, 2008: 222). The emerging information matrix has resulted in the need for a more collaborative and adaptive role of acquisitions within the library due to a proliferation in modes of access, along with the associated contingencies. With a multiplicity of formats in this matrix, it will be critical to move beyond rigid distinctions of "outmoded categories" (Plutchak, 2007: 82). Practice within the new information universe will depend on reconsidering the way that information is produced, used, and acquired.

References

ALCTS. 1994. "Statement on Principles and Standards of Acquisitions Practice." Acquisitions Section Ethics Task Force. Available: www.ala.org/ala/mgrps/divs/alcts/resources/collect/acq/acqethics.cfm (accessed October 15, 2009).

Burnette, Elizabeth S. 2008. "Budgeting and Acquisitions." In *Managing the Transition from Print to Electronic Journals and Resources: A Guide for Library and Information Professionals* (pp. 3–27), edited by Maria D. D. Collins and Patrick L. Carr. New York: Routledge.

Carr, Patrick L. 2008. "From Innovation to Transformation: A Review of the 2006–07 Serials Literature." *Library Resources and Technical Services* 53, no. 1: 3–14.

Chapman, Liz. 2004. *Managing Acquisitions in Library and Information Services*, rev. ed. London: Facet Publishing.

Lee, Hur-Li. 2000. "What Is a Collection?" *Journal of the American Society for Information Science* 52, no. 12: 1106–1113.

Manhoff, Marlene. 2006. "The Materiality of Digital Collections: Theoretical and Historical Perspectives." *portal: Libraries and the Academy* 6, no. 3: 311–325.

Plutchak, T. Scott. 2007. "What's a Serial When You're Running on Internet Time?" *The Serials Librarian* 52, no. 1/2: 79–90.

Pritchard, Sarah M. 2008. "Deconstructing the Library: Reconceptualizing Collections, Spaces and Services." *Journal of Library Administration* 48, no. 2: 219–233.

Propas, Sharon, and Vicky Reich. 1995. "Postmodern Acquisitions." *Library Acquisitions: Practice and Theory* 19, no. 1: 43–48.

Van Orsdel, Lee C. 2007. "The State of Scholarly Communication: An Environmental Scan of Emerging Issues, Pitfalls, and Possibilities." *The Serials Librarian* 52, no. 1/2: 191–209.

Chapter 3

Routes to Access

Finding a Path, Connecting with Content

Along with an expanded understanding of the information universe must come new premises regarding the nature of information transmission and the behavior of the end users who ultimately make use of that information upon discovery. A new and nuanced ontology of content is required to keep acquisitions a vital part of the emerging library and to move practices forward into the future. Such an ontological reformulation requires reframing the concept of "format" and the implications it has for the creation, discovery, and dissemination of content.

The linear-chain models of workflow described in the previous chapter are premised on two other assumptions regarding acquisitions' role in the provision of content, neither of which should be taken for granted any longer. The first assumption is that acquisitions will primarily be purchasing physical materials to add to the library's tangible collection. The outcome of this assumption is the construction of a workflow around the addition of physical items to a permanent collection. The physical item, therefore, becomes the driver of the process. The second assumption is that actual acquisitions practitioners are isolated from much of the service related to content provision within the library. This second assumption results in the theoretical and practical exclusion of acquisitions units from contributing to the greater service mission of the whole library. The end result of this line of thinking puts acquisitions in a single, fixed position within the larger information universe, namely procurement. Further, such a position threatens to keep acquisitions isolated *from* yet *within* the overall functioning of the library.

Item versus Format

Before making a decision about an acquisition, one must take into account *what* is being acquired. Certainly libraries will continue to buy books. However, since most libraries will not acquire *only* books, and not only *print* books, an approach is needed that does not start with thinking in terms of an item— "The Book"—but rather in terms of a format. Why is this subtle difference important? The key is that digital production, reproduction, delivery, and access have changed the rules quite a bit from the days when "a book was a book." New conceptions of and practices with information have changed the expectations of what roles both the library and end user play in the process.

Along the same lines that Manhoff (2006) argues for the materiality of digital objects, it is useful to revisit the idea of the *item* in the context of a library's sphere of access and the acquisitions process that contributes to the development of any given sphere. Rather than a physical container that has traditionally served as the carrier for content, it is appropriate to reconceive information in terms of its existence as an *object*: content that exists as something *material* but not necessarily *physical*. The idea of a collection needs to be approached not as items organized by formats but rather as formats that happen to be embodied as objects, which may or may not be physical entities. The implication is not that we have moved into a post-format environment where content is freed from its matrix of inscription. Indeed, the idea of stressing the importance of *the work* over *the document* is not an entirely new one (Smiraglia, 2003). Instead, we have moved from a vague *association* of format with a particular work to a more precise *practice* of format that capitalizes on the nuances that are inherent to the inscription of information objects. This is certainly driven by developments in the digital realm but does not suggest that an object is superior based only on its digital form, whatever that happens to be. Instead, we have a situation where the implications of an information object's "digitality" mean something substantially more than that it simply exists in an electronic format. Now, rather than items, the object of acquisitions is the *object*—the intersection of content and format.

What we have today that did not exist ten years ago is that in many cases access may be reliably established through a multiplicity of formats. This includes print books, of course, but may include other formats that are more appropriate for a given use. If we were to look at acquisitions in terms of formats instead of items, what would content look like? Figure 3-1 is an illustrative, but by no means comprehensive, model.

The model in Figure 3-1 allows an acquisitions practitioner to start thinking in terms of the format of content rather than the container of content. This is an essential difference from traditional acquisitions; the role of contemporary acquisitions is increasingly engaged with connecting to content no matter what its form, rather than buying an item regardless of its content.

Definition: **monograph**
Single complete textual work published as a comprehensive whole.

This approach challenges some basic tenets that have grounded past acquisitions practices. The notion that a book is a book—in other words, that a **monograph** is a printed book (Figure 3-2)— has served a structuring role in acquisitions practice.

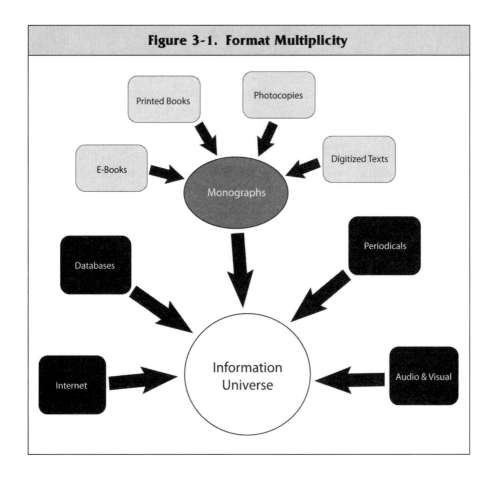

Figure 3-1. Format Multiplicity

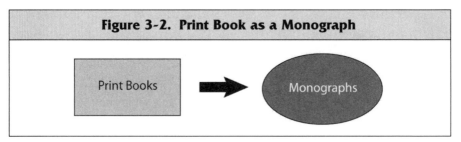

Figure 3-2. Print Book as a Monograph

Even the print-based model is not as straightforward as it first appears. Printed content does provide a number of options for acquisitions (Figure 3-3), which requires one kind of strategic

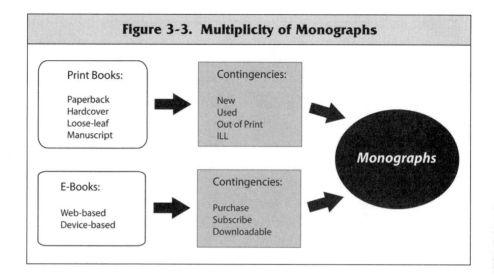

Figure 3-3. Multiplicity of Monographs

approach. Of course, the options for print formats are inevitably item based and therefore limited to actions that may be performed on or with a physical item. With print objects, though, a number of what can be thought of as "contingencies" occur, considerations that relate to their existence unique to them as physical objects. For example, contingencies might include print book availability (in stock, out of print, etc.), their condition (new, used, damaged), or any other factor that may affect their usability. Contingencies exist for electronic objects, too, but of an entirely different nature. Use of e-objects can be affected by how they are paid (subscription titles have an implied impermanence) or how they are accessed (through a PC or downloadable to a device). It is the growing number of format options and content configurations that have broken down the rigid structures that led to a highly efficient workflow in technical services. Simultaneously, however, these same available options and configurations have provided an incredible amount of flexibility within acquisitions practice.

Interestingly, this approach starts to blur some traditional lines of how content is handled by the library. If acquisitions starts to act on content objects to create a sphere of access, then the notion of acting on physical items to build a discrete collection no longer adequately defines the acquisitions function. This shift calls into question other traditional divisions, such as interlibrary loan and document delivery—which is typically considered part of access services. While in some ways this usual arrangement makes sense given the direct connection to library users and the separate software used for interlibrary loan requests, developing a model of acquisitions in the present day needs to work closely, if not directly, with those managing the interlibrary loan function. If acquisitions must be increasingly flexible to meet contemporary user needs and is working with content beyond a simple categorization of format, document delivery is, in fact, another route to access rather than a completely separate service.

The Case of E-books

Going into any acquisitions situation, practitioners will always have two options: to make content fit into item-based workflows or to have a flexible strategy that allows content to be acquired in any format. Unfortunately, the tendency is to approach acquisitions with a set workflow and attempt to make everything fit into it. Many electronic and consortial acquisitions do not fit nicely into the preestablished categories of traditional acquisitions.

Referring back to the main model (Figure 3-1), it is easy to see that within the broad traditional categories (monographs, journals, etc.), formats can vary quite a bit.

Definition: **e-book**

A text that is entirely available in electronic form. May be born digital or not.

These broad categories are analogous to how content is treated within the catalog: They reflect the *form* of the content rather than the format. In determining workflows, an electronic book, or **e-book**, has the form of a monograph—

textually, it might even be identical (e.g., PDF). With e-books, as with any format decision, trade-offs must be made; while physical books are a proven technology that both staff and patrons are used to, e-books provide speed of delivery, ease of access (including full-text searching), streamlined processing, and saving of shelf space. However, acquiring an e-book might be more like buying (or building) a database than like traditional book acquisitions. This is one place where the former approach to—and assumptions about—acquisitions could hamper organizations. It is unlikely that an e-book will fit exactly into a print book workflow.

Though the models for the publication and enhancement of e-books are finally stabilizing, this format still creates challenges in the acquisitions process. E-books are now available through several models, generally through an entity that is republishing material available from other publishers. For example, a title originally published in print from a university press might be available in e-book format from a different provider, likely with its own proprietary platform. Collections of e-books may be subscribed to through a model that allows access to predefined sets, perhaps with content that varies over time, of titles that the library does not own. Access is limited to a paid period of time, which, like most subscriptions, is usually a year. Content is accessed through an interface called a platform that allows for searching and display of content. E-book functionality may also provide access to multiple simultaneous users, off-site access, and enhanced features like bookmarking and note-taking.

In addition to, or instead of, the subscription model, there may be several routes to ownership of e-book content. One way is through package purchases directly from the e-publisher or through consortial agreements. These sets may be defined, for example, by subject and allow a critical mass of titles to be bought in perpetuity at a favorable price. In this instance, some of the selection has been done by the vendor, and the library may not have much (or any) input into *what* titles or *how many* are included in the package. Purchased titles are usually hosted by the publisher and likewise made available through a proprietary platform. However, unlike subscriptions, this content remains static.

E-books may also be purchased one at a time in many instances. Purchases can typically be made directly though the publisher or, increasingly, through monograph vendors. E-books from one or more e-publishers can be included in the profile of many approval plans, either for slip notification or for actual selection. Often the content is available for preview through the vendor's online database prior to purchase. Though purchased through a third party, these à la carte purchases are simply activated by the e-publisher and made available through the platform along with content that the library has subscribed to or purchased in a large content package through the publisher or a consortium (see Figure 3-4).

With several routes to access for e-books, the library has content acquisition options that can be adapted to many situations. So, too, is access available several ways. As with traditional

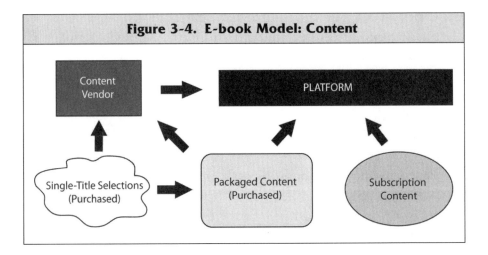

Figure 3-4. E-book Model: Content

books, a bibliographic record can be added to the library catalog. Unlike the traditional means of access, however, an embedded hyperlink can connect would-be readers directly to the e-book. Users access content directly through the e-book platform. The interface allows available e-book text to be searched like a database, either full-text or across specified fields. This creates a seamless, if complex, way for researchers to access digital content from many publishers via many routes (see Figure 3-5).

For the academic library, e-books are an exemplar of the promise and practicality of an enriched information universe. While not universally welcomed or accepted by students and scholars (Pyle, 2009), the ability to access, search, and annotate scholarly work from virtually anywhere should have a profound impact on the way that content can be used and information can be discovered. But as with any format options, there are trade-offs. Typically, printing and copying of an e-book's text is restricted to some degree in order to prevent unchecked reproduction of the content. The e-book format is

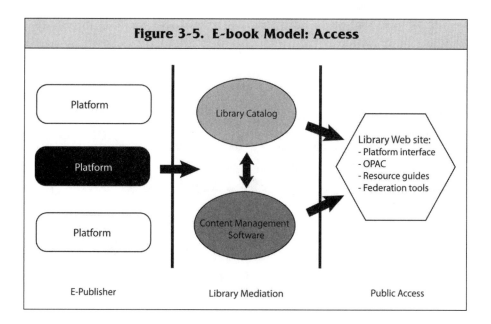

Figure 3-5. E-book Model: Access

Format Options

If a library lost its copy of the book *Writing and Difference* by Jacques Derrida, for example, and the philosophy selector made the decision to replace it, this would initiate a series of decisions. The selector may indicate that a hard-copy replacement is required, though it is simultaneously available as an e-book. This is the most basic function in acquisitions: buying an in-print book from a major academic publisher.

This is an example of a monograph purchase. Though there are other kinds of formats that could be described as monographs, a book is the exemplar of this category. Providing access to a monograph by way of adding printed books to the collection is what libraries have done most visibly, and the results generally meet library users' conditioned expectations. Additionally, since books have been a basically stable technology, even legacy processes for acquiring books are generally adequate.

Frequently, a contemporary academic library cannot fulfill its function simply by adding books to the shelves. Though having a collection of books that meets users' needs and expectations is critical when such a format is required and available, it is only one part of the mission—and the easiest part. For a library to succeed, all units within the organization must be ready and willing to adapt to end user expectations.

To be adaptable, it will help to keep the model above in mind. In a situation where a user is concerned primarily about the content, acquisitions can be less focused on the item. In the instance where it is not required that a physical book be added to the collection, it may be that a selector provides instructions to get the content in any format. It is in cases like these that being detached from an item-based workflow can be helpful. Now, one can start to think strategically about what to do next.

At this point, there may be several options because the imperative is no longer to "buy a book" but to get certain content as quickly as possible. Strategically, the *content object* may exist beyond the confines of a physical collection. Or perhaps the content is not even

(Continued)

> **Format Options** *(Continued)*
>
> to be added to the collection at all, as is the case with document delivery.The goal now is to bring certain content into the library's sphere of access, which may include used books or even electronic books, usually referred to as e-books. End use of content is a consideration not just for collection development practitioners but frequently for acquisitions practitioners as well.

not necessarily conducive to every kind of use, either. Doctorow (2008) notes that because of the propensity to multitask within the networked environment, the e-book format may not be well suited for reading long narratives (i.e., novels) on a computer screen. Though much of the resistance preventing a wider acceptance of e-books has been precisely the challenge of reading a long-format narrative, the improving technology of e-book readers is changing that attitude in the consumer market. Also, as with any emerging electronic technology, there is some question about the long-term stability of the content. Even if the purchased e-books were to be delivered in some form to the library, how would the content be made available without the interface provided by the publisher? However, while reliable access to e-books remains susceptible to disaster, so, too, does reliable access to print books.

Working with Vendors

Vendors provide favorable pricing and important services to acquisitions and, ultimately, to the library's users. Vendors are also a valuable resource for other kinds of services, such as providing information about forthcoming content products, troubleshooting technical difficulties, and structuring models of content acquisition that are customized for a particular library's situation. This means that the library's sphere of access is highly dependent on relationships with the content and service providers that make acquisitions both possible and successful. While technology mediates many interactions between acquisitions and the vendors they work with—whether the telephone, e-mail, or the Web—work with vendors is often done on a personal level. For librarians, having a designated contact in situations requiring a quick response can result in rapid problem solving. For example, if a requested book arrives damaged, a popular database goes down, or a quote for a major reference product is needed before the end of a fiscal year, being able to reach out to a specific someone on the vendor side can make a huge difference in terms of time. Vendor representatives, on the other hand, look to personal contacts in libraries to inform of upcoming products, work with during company restructuring, and contact about licensing, among many other functions. The personal quality of these professional relationships ensures that ongoing interactions in a changing information universe are efficient, meaningful, and mutually beneficial.

In working with vendors and publishers, it is essential to keep in mind at all times that business is—or potentially is—being conducted and that everyone involved should act accordingly. Even when interactions become friendly and informal, they should remain ethical. Of course, being professional does not preclude either friendliness or informality—in those cases where informality is appropriate. Vendors still invest a considerable amount in establishing and maintaining personal relationships with the libraries that they do—or might do—business with. The most obvious manifestation of that investment is sending out their representatives to meet with librarians and other interested parties in person. Often, such visits might seem like nothing more than sales calls and in some cases might be just that, but also provide an opportunity to interact with someone on a personal level. These visits should be viewed as opportunities to have the undivided attention of a company's agent. To capitalize on such opportunities, a librarian "accords a prompt and courteous reception insofar as conditions permit to all who call on legitimate business missions" (ALCTS, 1994, Statement 7). These visits can be an ideal situation to share with the vendor the library's service and content needs, a realistic outlook on resources, and the long-term strategic goals of the content acquisition plan. Once trust and rapport have been established, site visits and any subsequent negotiations need not be a "black box"—transparency will inevitably help both sides best reach their objectives. Instead, by communicating directly and honestly, librarians can then leverage the time that they have scheduled to work with a vendor to reach an outcome that is mutually beneficial. While this approach clearly applies to site visits from representatives, it applies as well to phone calls and even e-mail messages.

Since all relationships with vendors are predicated on the real or potential business that a library conducts with them, it is imperative that everyone involved "subscribes to and works for honesty, truth, and fairness in buying and selling, and denounces all forms and manifestations of bribery" (ALCTS, 1994, Statement 4). Decisions to work with particular vendors and publishers should be made objectively, to ensure that the fairest prices and best services are obtained on behalf of the library's users. In an effort to avoid any conflict of interest or favoritism, real or perceived, it is necessary that a librarian "declines personal gifts and gratuities" (ALCTS, 1994, Statement 5). As discussed in Chapter 2, it is important that the process for selecting a vendor in a given situation is equitable so that any decision results in the best value for the library and library user.

Online Acquisitions

In terms of speed and availability, the Web provides an enormous sphere of access as well as, in many cases, multiple routes to that access. While this is obvious on one level, availability and speed are not the only variables that go into developing a successful Web-based acquisitions strategy. Like other aspects of contemporary library work, new challenges are frequently defined in terms of abundance rather than the scarcity that defined collection-building strategies of past ages. Like any kind of information search, knowing *where* and *how* to find the most relevant sources remains an essential skill.

For an individual consumer, retail and auction sites on the Web may seem more or less interchangeable. When making library acquisitions, it is important to remember that not all Web retailers and auction sites are the same. The differences, though, may not be immediately apparent. These differences can be subtle, but should be thoroughly investigated before making any kind of Web site a regular source for content acquisition. Though a Web retailer may be selected because of a unique product offering, a choice may be driven, consciously or not, because of perceived convenience or familiarity rather than true appropriateness of the retailer for content acquisition. Like other acquisitions decisions, neither brand strength nor personal familiarity alone should predetermine a decision about a content supplier.

Prior to making any kind of acquisition through a Web retailer, the content need as identified by collection development should be assessed to ensure that the combination of content and service is best met with a particular route to access. Often, services that are marketed by the online retailer may also be provided by one of the library's established vendors. Any time necessary access can be brokered through a vendor, that route should be given priority. With the proliferation of formats and acquisition options, it is essential that acquisition and access be consolidated to whatever extent is possible. Working with a formal (or "traditional") library vendor allows for numerous advantages, including the potential for consolidated invoicing, substantial discounting, integrating content within the library's approval plan, and reducing shipping costs. Many vendors offer sophisticated inventory tracking through their online ordering interfaces, the same as many popular Web retailers, as well as the ability to work with publishers to **drop ship** items that are not stocked by the vendor.

If contingency makes the use of a Web retailer essential for providing access to content, it is important to know and understand the options

> *Definition:* **drop ship**
>
> When a vendor has a physical item sent directly from the publisher because the ordered item is not in stock. Material is still invoiced through the vendor.

that are available. The foremost consideration is that buying as an institution differs markedly from buying as an individual. The most important factor is whether a particular kind of acquisition is allowed by university or library policy. Some organizations, for example, may not permit purchases through an online auction site. If a staff member is using a Web site for library purchasing that might also be used for personal purchasing, separate accounts for library orders and payments will make library acquisitions easier to track and will prevent confusion later on. It is imperative to keep personal shopping completely separate from institutional purchasing to avoid inadvertently paying for personal items with library funds.

While not all Web retailers require a credit card in all cases, almost all such sites accept credit card payments. Again, the rules regulating credit card use vary significantly depending on the library or perhaps even the specific situation within a given library. Because of the inherent risk in using a credit card in the online environment, it is critical that purchasing rules are completely understood prior to making any kind of credit card payment. Such understanding does not necessarily diminish the institutional risk that goes along with using a credit card, but can minimize personal liability if a card number is compromised.

As with personal purchases, ensuring that a particular Web retailer is a reliable and trustworthy source makes common sense. For sites that are unfamiliar, checking with colleagues or requesting references via e-mail lists may provide some additional insight for doing business with such entities. Verifying that a site is secure (i.e., using encrypted transmission of sensitive data), usually identifiable by URLs prefaced with "https://," is another precaution that may be taken prior to transmitting credit card information. Documentation for credit card transactions is important, both for future reference and for audit situations. A copy of the Web receipt should be saved, if possible, and it may also make sense to attach any other supporting documentation that the online site mails or e-mails. Local requirements for tracking and approving such transactions should be understood ahead of making any kind of credit card expenditure.

Some larger Web retailers, especially those that routinely work with libraries in some capacity, may offer invoicing options that do not require the use of a credit card. Setting up an account with an alternative payment option may provide an opportunity to streamline acquisitions made from that site. However, not all of these arrangements are ultimately advantageous for the library. Just as for a library vendor, no payment plan should be established or used without making careful consideration about the long-term ramifications of such a decision. Thought should be given to aspects of the retailer's service that could, in turn, impact the library's service. Awareness of how content will be paid for is critical. The option to pay an invoice rather than paying from a monthly credit statement can make payments easier to process, and more frequent payments will ensure that library **encumbrances** are up to date. The ability to directly contact a

> *Definition:* **encumbrance**
> Funds reserved and tracked for an anticipated payment that have not yet been paid to a seller (i.e., expended).

representative at the retailer, by either phone or e-mail, for problem solving and having the opportunity to establish a relationship with service representatives at the company will make the inevitable problems easier to solve. Many sites provide interfaces that are relatively easy to use; however, when making multiple purchases on an ongoing basis, the service and feedback mechanisms that underlie the technical aspects of the Web site are the key to a retailer that will be supportive of acquisitions' role in the library. It is important to establish a service contact before a problem arises to ensure that a solution can be worked out expediently when necessary.

When going forward with purchases from Web sites, familiarity and habit can lead to oversight. Even minor mistakes will end up being costly for the library—whether in time, money, or both. When using online retailers for acquisitions, perceived convenience must be tempered with full consideration of the high transaction cost of keying in order information, paying the shipping and handling on single items, and documenting credit card expenditures. Processing orders one title at a time loses any economy of scale; the redundancy in data entry, shipping charges, and handling costs may add to actual cost of the order and opportunity costs in the additional time needed to process such orders. However, Internet sites can significantly broaden the content available to the library and supplement vendor services in important ways.

Archives: Present and Future

The archive is and, especially, *was* a place for keeping *things*. Even more than the usual library stacks, the archive was a place where the physical item went to be organized and, above all, preserved. Beyond books, the archive is a place for documents, papers, ephemera, and realia. Because it has been a place that defies conventional collecting practices, it has

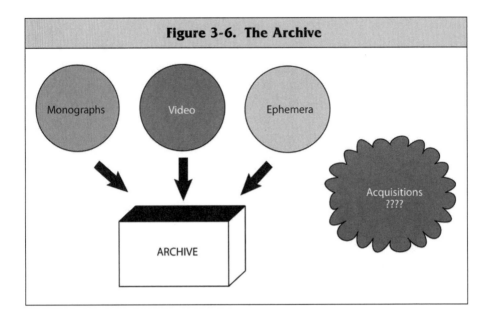

Figure 3-6. The Archive

remained largely independent of the conventional acquisitions workflow (Figure 3-6). Often, the acquisition of materials for the archive is done from within that unit, though occasionally acquisitions will support part or even all of the process.

This makes sense to a certain degree. If acquisitions is process oriented and the process is based on physical items, then the standardization of both the items and the process results in a smooth, even, and, above all, efficient flow of materials. Items destined for the archive are by definition exceptional. Like books, the archive is not going to disappear, become less important, or cease to encompass physical items. But like the book, the archive needs to be reconsidered vis-à-vis acquisitions.

Preservation has always been an element of collection building in libraries. Preservation plays a role in all aspects of the library's collection, from the books in the stacks to the materials in the archive. And acquisitions has always had a role to play in the long-term preservation of materials, especially in the evaluation and handling of new materials.

The reconceptualization of both archival practice and the role that acquisitions plays in preservation needs to come from an improved understanding of the information universe and a better sense of how the idea of format must operate separately from the idea of the item. Preservation can be thought of as a *practice* and the archive can be thought of as a *place*. While both have practical implications for the act of acquisition, neither concept provides a way of theorizing the process of acquisition.

When developing an acquisitions strategy, the key is to understand and develop an *archival trajectory* (Figure 3-7). Rather than the practice of preserving items or the place where

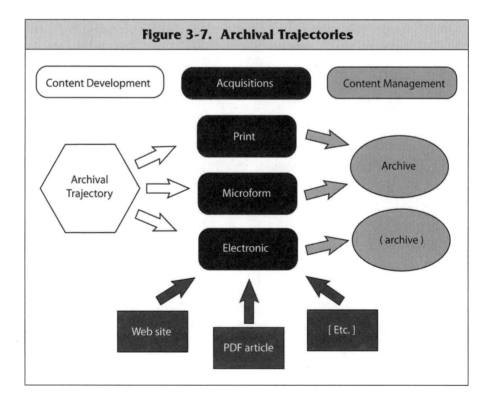

Figure 3-7. Archival Trajectories

items are stored, the archival trajectory is the *process* of acquiring formats in a way that meets the long-term needs of the collection and library users. Following through on the archival trajectory, like many aspects of service, requires close collaboration with other units within the library. In a practical sense, the notion of an archival trajectory is not new: Content is routinely acquired with an end use or end user in mind. However, if acquisitions participates in the process of determining and applying the archival trajectory, it is possible to effect a positive change in library practice. Where acquisitions is formally tasked to collaborate in the determination and projected use of content objects, a richer information environment may be created.

It is possible, though unlikely to be practical, that the object of acquisition for the archive would be handled by acquisitions. This is due to a key difference in the archival trajectory of the archive versus the general collection. The objects added to the archive tend to be singular in nature with an intrinsic worth that is only partially related to them as objects. More often than not, it is the contingencies surrounding that object—a special edition, a significant signature, a noteworthy owner—anything that sets one object apart from other, ostensibly similar objects and imbues it with singular value. Like acquiring a piece of art, the intrinsic uniqueness of a given item destined for the archive often makes the acquisition of such an object difficult to do separately from its identification and preservation. This is because the archival item is inherently conditional: The identification, acquisition, and preservation all depend on the conditions specific to a singular item. However, acquisitions will likely play an increasing role with *archival* material, such as the digital backups for electronic formats included in many purchases. In cases where access is mediated by acquisitions, such a role is vital to make sure that content is delivered and stored correctly. The exact nature of the role is highly contingent on the publisher, the content, the intended use, and long-term needs, among other variables.

In those cases where acquisitions is working with and for the archive, format and container will once again overlap. Information objects will also be artifacts. The singularity possessed by these items will make them rare and exceptional, and that has implications for acquiring them. For one, identifying if an item is available and where it might be found (not to mention at what price) may take additional time. Also, such rarities are not likely to be available through mainstream library vendors. A host of online sources and resources can make the job easier but are, again, exceptional even by contemporary acquisitions standards and may involve extensive personal communication and the highest standards of verification that the material is what was represented. For books, local dealers may have something on hand or know how to get them. More likely than not, however, such rarities are not locally procurable. Specialty Web sellers, such as Alibris (www .alibris.com) or the seller network accessible via Amazon.com, can provide a quick overview of availability and price. For specialty items, especially those items that are not books, eBay (www.ebay.com) may be a good place to look. Though some of these routes are familiar to many acquisitions practitioners through their personal experience, it is essential to remember that extra consideration may be required when purchasing library content from these sites.

Besides price, however, such purchases conceal some hidden costs. Time invested in searching, placing orders, and evaluating materials upon arrival can be considerable. Especially given that some descriptions online may be less than forthcoming about critical defects to an object, the library takes on some risk purchasing these materials sight unseen; return policies from Web vendors can vary greatly, from the very accommodating to the nonexistent. Shipping and handling costs of such materials may be quite high, and might go even higher if the material needs to be insured—which is almost always an additional cost, when an option at all. In the end, the library may need to track down and purchase a second item, if that is an option, when the condition or bottom-line price of the first item falls outside the acceptable parameters for the library.

One of the most engaging aspects of acquisitions is working with rare, unique, or other special materials. Such acquisitions require some planning before starting out and a solid grasp of what is being sought for the collection, especially the archival trajectory for such items. In this case, the information object becomes a unique, nonreproducible artifact where the medium, so to speak, is the message. While rewarding for the acquisitions professional, the full institutional cost in terms of time and money for such a transaction needs to be taken into account.

"Free": Costs and Considerations

Acquisitions is typically associated with the purchasing of materials. This makes sense, since libraries typically must pay for the information that they provide access to. However, the association of acquisitions only with the processing of paid orders reduces the acquisitions function to something rote and clerical, and diminishes the strategic potential of the acquisitions practitioner in perceived or real terms.

Any academic acquisitions operation interacts with free material in at least several arenas. The notion of the term "free" here mitigates the perceived impact that these interactions actually have. Four common areas of encounter with free materials are gifts or donated materials, open-access publications, locally produced content, and exchange programs. While constituting a small portion of the information universe, these materials may have a disproportionate draw on staff time and resources and must be accounted for in terms of personnel, computing, and storage. Including these categories of free content in the conceptualization of the acquisitions function requires a different kind of thinking.

Materials that come in as random donations can take considerable time to manage. Such random donations may or may not be accepted by the library, then may or may not go to acquisitions. The costs need to be carefully considered; processing content will take time, and storing the content, regardless of its format, will take up space of some kind. Even the opportunity cost—what does not get done at the expense of acting on the free content—should be a factor in deciding what to add. Finally, access to any content will need to be managed for the long term. If it is not feasible to provide systematic and stable access to a particular information object, it is probably better not to act on it. Like all aspects of acquisitions work, any consideration given to such gifts should be part of a broader strategy for actively managing the library's sphere of access. As with other content to which the library wishes to provide access, an acquisitions strategy developed for donations needs to be part of a wider content development program. It is also worthwhile to note that not everything that comes in without an order is a donation. Sometimes unscrupulous publishers will send content that was not ordered in hopes of being able to invoice for it at a later time. Occasionally, an invoice will be included in hopes of tricking the person receiving content at the library into paying for something that was not formally selected.

The OA movement (discussed previously) has gained momentum in recent years and has some uncertain implications for both the publishing and library worlds. Content available on the Web as an OA resource will not be acquired the same way that a paid resource would be. However, if such a resource is intentionally brought into the library's sphere of access, the resource could potentially impact acquisitions. For example, the availability of an OA resource might result in the cancellation of a print publication. While the OA title would not necessarily need to be acquired, the print title would still need to be canceled with the vendor. Acquisitions may also have to manage part of the library's access as a matter of routine e-resource maintenance.

Other routes are available to utilize resources differently in a way that expands the library's sphere of access to various kinds of materials. One such route is through an **exchange program**, where the library trades some material (e.g., duplicate items or locally published content) for other content that may be difficult to locate or pay for. This can be an effective strategy for dealing with countries

> *Definition:* **exchange program**
>
> A program set up between two or more libraries where content is traded among participants.

or regions where publishing is inconsistent, where lack of infrastructure poses barriers to long-distance business, or the exchange partner has locally produced content that is of interest but not available for sale. Exchanges can also occur between libraries within the same region if they are trying to collect specialized subject content that is generally difficult to obtain. Exchanges, however, can be time consuming to set up and administer and should be monitored to ensure that the library is getting out of the plan what is being invested in it (Chapman, 2004). Like blanket plans (see Chapter 2), exchange programs may be highly rewarding in terms of rare or ephemeral materials, but may require a great deal of time to administer.

Conclusion: Ensuring Connectivity

One of the only ways to overcome the proliferation of formats and user preferences is to build versatility into the acquisitions process. This can be accomplished by cross-training staff and structuring the ordering process as efficiently as possible. Maintaining a variety of work flows is necessary to a degree, but steps should be standardized where possible. Also, establishing and maintaining effective, professional relationships with vendors will help ensure that routes to access are maximized.

It is critical that collection building in libraries moves away from dichotomies such as "print-or-electronic" and "ownership-or-access." Polarities such as these were useful for structuring discussions around the early Internet or nascent digitization technologies. However, with the maturing of the Web and the evolving best practices for digital content creation and conversion, the responsibility of ensuring access is best met with an array of options rather than a fixed course of action. One way of meeting this challenge is by reevaluating the notion of format and its implications within the matrix of scholarly communication.

Versatility will depend on the use of technology as an adaptable tool rather than an absolute limit. And technology will need to be employed creatively at all stages of scholarly communication. The further development of today's e-book platforms into multimedia content solutions will free acquisitions from dependence on tangible-format media and allow for more accessible, flexible modes of access to nontextual information objects. However, print and other tangible media will continue to have an important role in the assurance of library user connectivity to content. Publisher use of advanced print-on-demand technology has the potential to essentially end the notion of items being out of print, allowing text in digital format to be converted into print and acquired through established vendors whenever needed (Thatcher, 2009). Finally, acquisitions must be prepared to adapt available technology to solve some of the puzzles created in the new information universe. For example, it may be possible to track electronic standing orders by creatively using publisher Really Simple Syndication (RSS) feeds rather than tracking new releases manually (Arch, 2009). An RSS feed will allow the publisher to notify acquisitions automatically when a new volume has been made available online in cases where an item is not delivered to the library. Another possible use of technology is the emerging ONIX for Publications Licenses (ONIX-PL) standard that "is part of a family of XML formats for the communication of licensing terms" for digital resources (www.editeur.org/21/ONIX-PL/) .ONIX-PL is intended to facilitate licensing and management of electronic resources. For libraries, such a standard could streamline the acquisition and licensing of content through the use of an electronic resource management system, or ERMS (discussed in Chapter 4). Such creative use of technology provides options that allow decisions to be made based on, rather than limited by, available formats.

Acquisitions plays a keystone role in connecting people with content. While this has always been the case, in the past, ensuring connectivity could be equated with locating, ordering, and paying for physical items. Increasingly, the role that acquisitions plays in ensuring access takes on many forms and must be done at a higher level. While a growing number of electronic formats has increased the available options for providing access, content inscribed within tangible formats (e.g., print books) remains an important part of developing the library's sphere of access. As more formats with different ordering, access, and maintenance requirements emerge, acquisitions work will inevitably only become more nuanced and complex. However, these often disparate-seeming tasks that typically fall to acquisitions can likewise be fitted systematically into a broader paradigm of ensuring access that must necessarily replace an outmoded approach based on buying books. Such an environment requires a collaborative and outcome-focused approach rather than one that is purely process-based.

References

ALCTS. 1994. "Statement on Principles and Standards of Acquisitions Practice." Acquisitions Section Ethics Task Force. Available: www.ala.org/ala/mgrps/divs/alcts/resources/collect/acq/acqethics.cfm (accessed October 15, 2009).

Arch, Xan. 2009. "RSS for Acq." *Against the Grain* 21, no. 2: 59–60.

Chapman, Liz. 2004. *Managing Acquisitions in Library and Information Services*, rev. ed. London: Facet.

Doctorow, Cory. 2008. *Content: Selected Essays on Technology, Creativity, and the Future of the Future*. San Francisco, Tachyon.

Manhoff, Marlene. 2006. "The Materiality of Digital Collections: Theoretical and Historical Perspectives." *portal: Libraries and the Academy* 6, no. 3: 311–325.

Pyle, Encarnacion. 2009. "OSU Book Winnowing Opposed." *Columbus Dispatch*, May 13, 2009. Available: www.dispatch.com/live/content/local_news/stories/2009/05/13/OSU_library.ART_ART_05-13-09_B1_ITDRI8J.html (accessed June 24, 2009).

Smiraglia, Richard P. 2003. "The History of 'The Work' in the Modern Catalog." *Historical Aspects of Cataloging and Classification* 35, no. 3/4: 553–567.

Thatcher, Sanford G. 2009. "The Hidden Digital Revolution in Scholarly Publishing: POD, SRDP, the 'Long Tail,' and Open Access." *Against the Grain* 21, no. 2: 60–63.

Chapter 4

Service and Feedback

The Functional Role of Acquisitions

When one thinks of acquisitions, perhaps what most often comes to mind is buying books. While it may be true that acquisitions does, in fact, buy books for the library collection, the critical function of acquisitions is not simply the purchase of materials. Acquisitions is a service-oriented unit of the library and serves the community of library users to the same degree that other areas of the library do. However, acquisitions has a kind of invisible aspect to it. While the idea of the physical collection is the most tangible and pervasive image of the library, the service value added by acquisitions is not as immediately apparent as the value added by other service areas of library such as reference, circulation, or even cataloging. Yet, bringing content into a library's sphere of access (see Chapters 2 and 3) adds a tremendous amount of value since the content is otherwise unavailable—and perhaps even unknown. However, much as the business of acquisitions is not as straightforward as simply buying books, its transformation is, likewise, nothing as simple as getting access. Acquisitions, like all other parts of the library, is a service sector that adds value by *acting* on content and *interacting* with the library, campus, and other communities of which it is a part.

81

Libraries through the ages became very efficient at building and organizing physical collections of items. This ensured a certain availability of what was, hopefully, a critical mass of content that could be physically accessed when needed. When libraries consisted of physical items, collection building was largely anticipatory. Physical items necessarily had to be identified, then moved in some kind of physical form to a physical location where a patron could, quite literally, pick an item up. Libraries functioned as some of the most efficient information-gathering machines of the previous, mechanical age. The collecting of books and journals, especially, and the indexes and abstracts that were required to locate specific pieces of information buried within them are ingenious methods of searching print-bound information. The nature of the physical-item container impacted all library services, to be sure, but had the greatest implication for acquisitions, which dealt almost entirely with the container. Those tasked with locating content did not necessarily have to identify where information was printed, but had to discover where the objects were located. Looking at the library in terms of its physicality, some structural categories can be readily identified and used to help illustrate the various service areas.

The first of these broad categories includes library functions that are primarily content based. One area of librarianship organized primarily, though perhaps not exclusively, around content is collection development. When doing collection development, the first priority is to *identify* the content—the specific, organized information—that is needed. Content might include the text of a novel or the music from a particular recital. Typically, this identification of content has occurred simultaneously with the identification of an item (e.g., book or CD). The second part of the collection development function is *selection* of the content for the collection. Such a selection will be based on a number of factors, but ultimately will have a hypothetical end user in mind. This selection of content will likely continue to be tied to format (e.g., e-book or standard CD), but developing a collection—physical, virtual, or just-in-time—will foremost be concerned with content.

Another content-based function of library services is the provision of reference service. The goal of reference service is to first facilitate discovery of content and then help determine how to establish access. This is in response to an acute information need, where learning the information is of primary importance. The format, the vehicle to discovery, will be an essential consideration in terms of timely access, but is ultimately ancillary to the user's information needs.

While the acquisition of content necessarily includes work with content at some level, it is not the organizing principle of the acquisitions function (see Figure 4-1).

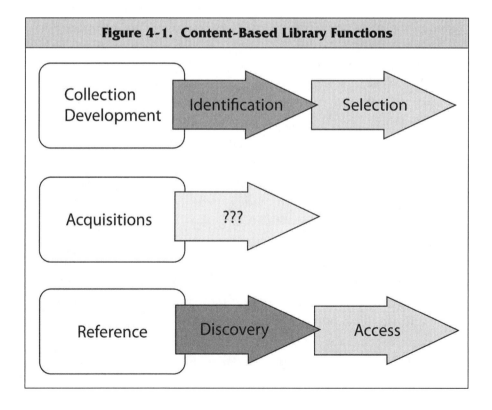

Figure 4-1. Content-Based Library Functions

At the same time, other service functions within the library are process based. One of these functions is circulation. The circulation process may first be defined in terms of policy, which defines what items circulate, for how long, and to whom. For example, a policy might indicate that all materials in a collection circulate except those designated as being part of reference or special collections. From the regime of general policies establishing the use of materials, specific procedures are established. Procedures may detail how a book is checked out, how the borrowing period is determined, and what penalties are invoked when a borrowing period is exceeded. A procedure might specify that students may check out circulating books for 28 days or that faculty members may check out reference items for two days. The circulating of items is indifferent to the content but also in a large degree equally indifferent to the container, as well; it is, rather, organized around the process for temporarily changing the possession of containers and tracking that possession.

A second process-based library function is cataloging. The procedure for cataloging is well established with national standards (e.g., *Anglo-American Cataloguing Rules*, Second Edition, or AACR2) that dictate how content objects should be treated generally. It is prescribed, for example, that the title is transcribed from the title page into the 245 field of the MARC record; transcription includes specific instructions for setting indicators, creating subfields, and even the use of capitalization. Because the procedure is set for all catalogers, the local policies are derived from the procedure. Examples of local cataloging policy include identifying those situations when local notes are added to the record to enrich description or when additional custom fields of description are used to meet user needs. While intellectual reconfigurations of cataloging (e.g., Functional Requirements for Bibliographic Records) foreshadow the reprioritization of content within the cataloging function, one that gives content an even higher priority in the cataloging process, the function of cataloging itself has hitherto centered on structuring a *process* for description of content items as an *organizing principle*. While subject heading assignment and classification are undoubtedly functions focused on the content, these practices are done within the framework of describing an item.

Though the acquisition of library content has included local processes, it is not based on process in the same way as access services or cataloging (Figure 4-2).

This leaves the need for a third category to represent the traditional organizing approach to acquisitions. While all aspects of service within the modern library have been influenced by the *item*, the acquisitions function is uniquely centered on the

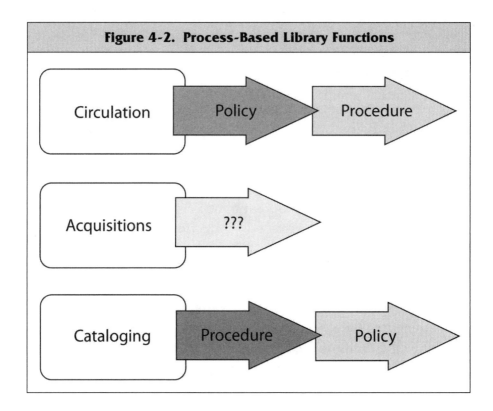

Figure 4-2. Process-Based Library Functions

Circulation — Policy → Procedure

Acquisitions — ??? →

Cataloging — Procedure → Policy

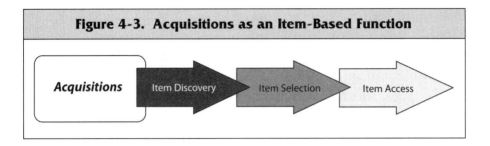

Figure 4-3. Acquisitions as an Item-Based Function

item as a basic essence of its being—the item is, therefore, an *ontological* entity. What emerges in item-based acquisitions functions is a routine that starts with an *item*—assumed to be a *physical entity*—and then bases all subsequent functions on that fact (see Figure 4-3). Acquisitions has had to act on items in a unique way, where they were not primarily the manifestation of a procedure (generally) nor the embodiment of content (specifically).

Aspects of Service

As new formats continue to proliferate in the new information universe, adding *objects* even while neutralizing *items*, acquisitions needs to reposition itself conceptually within the information universe and functionally in the library. Part of the complexity is that physical items continue to exist within the collection and as potential objects to be acquired. In specific cases, such as rare book collections, physical items even maintain their primacy. It may be, and likely should be, impossible to concentrate on physicality or format as a starting point for rethinking acquisitions. Rather, conceptions of service should be framed in acquisitions according to new demands by patrons and the supply of content. Anderson (2007), for example, has made the case for developing patron-centered practices that become possible in acquisitions with the erosion between technical and public services. He argues that any approach to acquisitions must be thought of in terms of serving library users "*directly* by being flexible and responding to their changing needs" (Anderson, 2007: 190; emphasis original). Such changes in content production and consumption are driving changes in the organization of acquisitions, too, leading to a range of responses when reorganizing technical services. Adaptation might involve any number of changes. One such change might result in reimagining the acquisitions librarian as the e-resources librarian, if appropriate to the mission of the library, the content being acquired, and the time needed to manage various resources. Other, more drastic responses might result in merging acquisitions with other library units or disbanding the formal acquisitions unit altogether in favor of a more streamlined or integrated technical services organization (Lopatin, 2004). Unless the library is foregoing all continuing and new acquisitions, however, the professional competency of acquisitions must reside somewhere in the organization and be readily identifiable. No matter the response to the growing instability within the new information universe, acquisitions work is only getting more complicated. Acquisitions functions must be reevaluated as its own discrete element of overall library services no matter how the functions of acquiring content are ultimately manifested organizationally.

The most important aspect of reconsidering acquisitions as a *function* (as opposed to acquisitions as an *organizational unit*) is to ensure that the function is defined in terms of *service* rather than process. In fact, no matter how the tasks are divided, it is important to define what exactly is being designated as acquisitions work. A key in this approach is to note that due to the organizational contingencies mentioned above, it may be impossible to define things that acquisitions does that no other service or administrative unit in the library or the university might do; indeed, acquisitions may do all of

Potential Access

Acquisitions foremost provides the *potential* for access, and may achieve this in many ways. It is important to note that collection development defines access needs, cataloging creates the pathway for access, reference creates the interface for access, and access services brokers or mediates the access. This potential for access is generated in a number of functions, such as the following:

- Managing vendor relationships
- Placing, tracking, and following up on orders
- Reviewing, transmitting, and filing licenses
- Receiving orders and establishing access to e-resources
- Monitoring the budget and reporting balances
- Paying invoices, balancing credit card statements, and processing seller-issued credits

As described in Chapter 3, acquisitions actively creates a sphere of access that has traditionally been considered to be the collection— those items that are owned by the institution. However, the sphere of access might include virtual electronic resources to which the library has access or other content that is mediated by the library but not added to a permanent collection.

these or none (in the cases where there is no separate acquisitions unit).

With access to content as a central goal, service from the library can be modeled in terms of access. When such a model is created, the traditional notion of the supply chain or static channel of information dissemination breaks down. While the model of the supply chain still retains some use, content that is object- rather than item-driven is not as fixed and can be acted on in different ways. In most circumstances, it can be useful to conceptualize routes to access as being like a "cloud" rather than distinct, predetermined paths to follow in connecting with con-

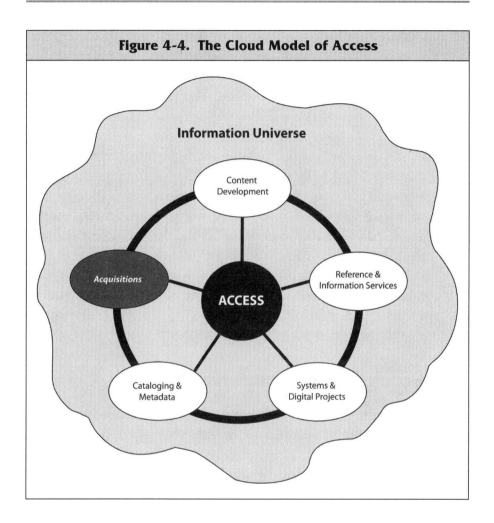

Figure 4-4. The Cloud Model of Access

Information Universe

Content Development

Acquisitions

ACCESS

Reference & Information Services

Cataloging & Metadata

Systems & Digital Projects

tent (Figure 4-4). A model focused on service positions acquisitions along with other units of the library and emphasizes a shared approach to providing access. Such a model underscores the breakdown of fixed boundaries between traditional library units already well underway (Bosch, Promis, and Sugnet, 2005). Such a service imperative drives a collaborative approach to acquisitions whether it is the immediate curricular needs of the liberal arts environment or the long-term, subject-intensive needs of the research environment.

More than ever, the conception of service as part of the acquisitions function should be framed foremost according to new demands created by the diversity of student, faculty, and researcher needs and expectations. This suggests a fluid notion of content that meets these new demands with a nuanced supply of information available from a field potential of formats. While acquisitions professionals still must hold to the standard that they strive "consistently for knowledge of the publishing and bookselling industry" (ALCTS, 1994, Statement 10), complete knowledge of publishing output is not possible. Instead, acquisitions practitioners must be ready to locate content through the tools at hand such as vendors (including approval plans), sophisticated use of the Web, and the assistance of innovative colleagues. Acquisitions must be able to meet access needs of information age library users by bringing necessary information objects into the library's sphere of access.

Acceleration: Disintermediation

The current state of publishing has created a paradox. On the one hand, mainstream search technologies such as Google, Amazon.com, and other full-text search products seem to be rapidly disintermediating information seeking at all levels. Almost anyone can enter some keywords and generate a somewhat usable list of results, whether using a free online search engine or an expensive, library-supported resource. At the same time, the vastly expansive information universe is so complicated and chaotic that even experienced information seekers find themselves quickly overwhelmed. At once there is both a plethora of information that can be found almost immediately and, simultaneously, a huge amount of information that may remain elusive even after several refined searches.

The role of the academic librarian has been reasserted within this new landscape where information "noise" may seem everywhere while sought-after content seems nowhere. This new information universe has posed challenges across the entire library. Acquisitions is actually called to mediate in two distinct parts of the access process. In the first instance, acquisitions practitioners increasingly must be able to identify the location— real or virtual—of more content from more sources in a variety of formats. In the second instance, acquisitions practitioners may need to maintain the access after it has been successfully established. The latter situation was represented to a degree when all content was in a physical format: Acquisitions practitioners would often have to replace lost materials or add additional copies of extremely popular material. However, this was a relatively rare occurrence and, being part of the more general acquisition of physical items, was practically automatic. In addition to these physical items, there is now an added layer of technology in the form of resource management software as well as various electronic formats that might require active management and upkeep.

In the end, successful disintermediated access requires a high degree of mediation behind the scenes. The function of acquisitions within the library has expanded and is now a technology-driven, multivalent task. Where the potential for access within the acquisitions unit could once be generated through a number of essentially clerical functions—phone calls, mail order, faxes, and filing—the role of acquisitions is now complicated by expectations of around-the-clock, real-time access to an information base many times larger than anything that could be imagined before the dawning of the information age. It is impossible now to remove the practice of acquiring content from the practice of providing information service to the library patrons. These aspects of service create the first half of a two-part cycle, where service is directly tied to library user needs in real time, and user needs in real time reinforce aspects of service.

The multiple routes available to content require heavily mediated access controls. A suite of software tools may be used by acquisitions to maintain access, including the following:

- Integrated library system (ILS)
- Electronic resource management system (ERMS)
- A-to-Z list
- Link resolver
- Vendor online database
- Institutional repository (IR) and LOCKSS (Lots of Copies Keep Stuff Safe, as part of the archival trajectory)

These electronic tools have many forms and often require complex, technical, and even proprietary specifications to run. It may be that acquisitions administers all, some, none, or just parts of these systems. Most of these systems will be implemented and run in close collaboration with the library systems unit or the university information technology department. However, the information that goes into and comes out of these systems will inevitably involve acquisitions once they are in place. Because these information systems are implemented to manage the content that the library has access to, data concerning acquisitions details—such as payment amount, license terms, package content, and consortial agreements—will inevitably be needed for system enrichment or report verification. A critical consideration when developing, evaluating, streamlining, or updating an acquisitions unit or its workflow is knowing how these tools can be used, if at all, in improving service to library users as provided by acquisitions. Such an evaluation will be site specific, determined in part by local needs and availability of resources.

Such technology-driven tools, however, contribute just as much to the changing nature of acquisitions work as does the changing nature of information itself. Just as a nuanced understanding of formats is required to respond adequately to library user needs, technical expertise is required to successfully manage an acquisitions program in an academic environment. The biggest impact, perhaps, is the concentration of work in higher level positions. Tasks that once could be delegated to entry-level paraprofessionals or detail-oriented students, including transmission of orders, processing claims, or entering payment information, are increasingly automated by way of complex software. This is true not only for the ILS but for some of the other systems that may fall to acquisitions, such as an ERMS. Some systems, such as the vendor's online ordering system, may not be administered by the library but may interface with one or more library systems to deliver MARC records, receive orders, or transmit invoice data. In some cases, the acquisitions professional will need to partner closely with the systems librarian or even the university information technology office. Of course, the technological knowledge may reside in acquisitions, streamlining part of the process. Any system that acquisitions uses to manage content objects, orders, or invoices will require some kind of trade-off. Sometimes this can be as simple as getting detailed training to maximize the use of the system. Other times, it can require establishing relationships to ensure an appropriate level of technical support. In all cases, the implementation and impact of any management system will likely have to be presented to colleagues and administrators in terms of some metric that demonstrates added value. Value can be determined many ways, but savings (e.g., time or money) or enhanced service (e.g., reduced time between ordering and access) are two ways to measure the value of a technology tool.

The Integrated Library System

Because of its ubiquity, the ILS is likely to be familiar to most library staff no matter where they work. Still occasionally referred to erroneously as the online catalog (which actually forms just one part of the ILS), these systems continue to be the primary locus of acquisitions work where they have been set up. Though not all libraries use an ILS to manage the acquisitions process, such a system can leverage technology to organize, integrate, and streamline essential functions. The ILS facilitates four critical acquisitions functions: placing and maintaining orders, recording receipts, tracking payments and funds, and storing vendor information. In cases where acquisitions adds and maintains bibliographic records, work with the ILS will be even more extensive. Since it is the system from which the online catalog is generated, it is the logical place to track the ordering and receipt of orders for content purchased or leased by the library.

Along with the content and the associated orders that acquisitions is working with, vendor and fund information is usually entered in the system as well. At its most basic, the ILS improves upon a file-based strategy for managing orders, a Rolodex-based system for tracking vendor contact information, and a calculator-based technology for tracking fund information. But strategically, the ILS needs to be conceived of, and subsequently utilized, beyond the notion of information storage. The contemporary ILS, whether commercial or open source, is a dynamic database that provides powerful tracking and reporting capabilities that frequently can be automated, at least to a degree. Automating the ILS where possible can absorb redundant tasks, such as creating online orders, and free up time to address more difficult problems.

The Electronic Resource Management System

The ERMS has been developed to fill a resource management need not met by the traditional ILS, even in those systems with a robust acquisitions module. The reason is that the current practice of electronic resource acquisition is more complicated than can be effectively handled by ILS architecture. The

ERMS evolved out of the spreadsheets and paper files that librarians started in order to track those things that could not be added in a systematic way to the ILS: license terms, service inquiries, access requirements, and renewal dates. ERMSs have been developed by all the major commercial ILS vendors, though most are intended to be sold as separate modules. Of course, an ERMS that "matches" a library's ILS will more fully integrate the two databases of information. In particular, the ability to have the financial information shared by both systems is what makes the addition of an ERMS particularly useful. Frequently, however, it is integrating the financial data from the two systems that forms one of the largest challenges and severely limits the utility of the ERMS. Another consideration in starting up an ERMS alongside the ILS is the sheer amount of time it takes to get electronic resource data entered into the ERMS. The ERMS will, in the final analysis, only be as good as the data that have been put into it. This alone restricts the number of libraries that can afford to get an ERMS fully functional.

A promising solution for managing electronic resources is agent-supplied online systems. Basically extensions of current online agent databases (e.g., EBSCONET, SwetsWise, OttoSerials, etc.), such systems offer similar advantages to those online systems developed by large monographic vendors. Like monographic acquisitions, including firm, standing, and approval orders, which can be effectively and efficiently managed through a given vendor's online system, subscription agents' online systems may prove to be the best way to keep on top of electronic resource orders of all kinds, including e-journals, packages, and consortial purchases. While the role of the serial agents was seriously in doubt when publisher-direct packages and publisher-bundled "big deals" seemed to be the direction of journal publishing, the importance of agent-mediated subscription is becoming clear. Subscription agents already possess a large amount of pertinent

Do You Need an ERMS?

It may seem that an electronic resource management system will solve much of the work and streamline much of the processing that goes into acquiring and managing electronic resources. Especially in acquisitions, where securing access has become quite complicated for many resources, a technological tool that promises the possibility of organization and streamlining may be quite tempting.

As with many technologies, an ERMS will not automatically simplify the e-resource management complications that seem to appear at every stage of the process.

Some goals to have in mind at the start of the evaluation process include the following:

- Know what functions the ERMS will need to have to save time in acquisitions.
- Know the technical limits of any ERMS under consideration.
- Know the limits of your organization's technical knowledge and determine how those limits will impact implementation and maintenance. (If the ERMS under consideration is open source, make sure that there is time and expertise available within the organization to support the system before it is implemented.)
- Know to what extent the ERMS will need to interact with your ILS.
- Know exactly how the ERMS will be used within and in support of the acquisitions workflow.
- Know what people or units outside acquisitions will need access to the ERMS and how administration of the system will be managed.

(Continued on facing page)

subscription information within their own databases, such as pricing, subscription periods, up-to-date publisher contact information, and claiming history, which makes the subsequent tracking of this information redundant if the library is merely

Do You Need an ERMS? *(Continued)*

- Know what kinds of experiences other libraries have had with the ERMS products under consideration.

- Know what level of customer support is available from the ERMS provider. (If the ERMS under consideration is open source, make sure that a process is in place to communicate problems and develop solutions before the system is implemented.)

Keep in mind that the ERMS is likely to be just one system supporting just one part of the library's acquisitions functions. The trade-offs must be carefully considered and the decision to invest an organization's time and money in the implementation and maintenance of such a system must be made only when an ERMS will result in a net savings.

Some questions to have in mind before going ahead with buying and implementing an ERMS are these:

- Will the cost of purchase and ongoing maintenance take away from other products or services that could simplify or improve the work being done in acquisitions?

- Does the added value from working with an ERMS justify the cost of the product and its upkeep?

- Is there a critical mass of e-resources that justifies the need for a specialized management system?

Like any tool, the ERMS will be helpful to a widely varying degree. Determining organizational need, available resources for implementation and support, and the long-term plan for integrating the ERMS into the acquisitions function will ensure that use of the system is appropriate and productive.

reentering the data. Though not as robust as a stand-alone ERMS module, such agent-based subscription management systems can provide a convenient and economical means of tracking e-resources along with print subscriptions.

Such a system is not a panacea. By relying on such a vendor system, the library must essentially depend on the vendor to maintain the system and provide continuous, reliable access. This may not matter, as much of the same monograph data has been similarly outsourced (perhaps to an even greater extent) through vendor online databases. Information does get back to the library in terms of renewal lists and invoices. However, if the subscription and consortial management data were to be tracked through a given vendor, the library would be tied to that vendor. While not requiring a business relationship that goes on ad infinitum, the implications for changing vendors in this circumstance would be significant. Though it may be possible to use emerging ERMS standards to walk data from a vendor's database to the library's ERMS, an agreement should be worked out ahead of time with the vendor to ensure the portability of the library's data. Also, some organizations may not allow their data to be hosted by a third party. In that case, the library might be required to purchase an ERMS that can be maintained on site if such functionality is important to managing access to e-resources.

Other Systems

Given the likely large number of databases and inevitable overlap of holdings, two systems have emerged to manage access. While not necessarily designed for management of acquisitions or by an acquisitions department, these systems are an almost ubiquitous part of the access regime. The *A-to-Z list* provides a means of providing access to databases via an online list. The *link resolver* allows the library user to collocate and access all instances of content available from multiple online sources on the fly. Finally, *federated searching* is a technology that enables a library user to run a given search simultaneously across many products and interfaces to decrease search time and collocate results.

While none of these technologies is directly part of an acquisitions function, access considerations permeate all aspects of the overarching library service mission. It is possible that any number of the acquisitions functions will involve, or at least intersect, with one or more of these technologies. For libraries that offer access to large amounts of online content, these management tools are a critical part of service. As the service imperative increases for acquisitions, knowing how content can be managed to best provide routes to access for end users is a critical aspect of the function.

Mechanisms of Feedback

Along with the ever-increasing routes to access, ever-expanding mechanisms of feedback have proliferated throughout both technological and cultural space. The idea of feedback has become familiar through its ubiquity; such mechanisms permeate daily life. Feedback may be used on Web retail and auction sites, informally through blog posts and "tweets," solicited through online surveys, or even work in less definite and unintentional ways. E-mail and social networking provide a constant flow of communication between peers and colleagues, and with it a barrage of feedback information. Libraries may even rely on feedback from highly specialized survey instruments such as the Association of Research Libraries' LibQUAL+ (www.libqual.org). These mechanisms serve a regulating function for both services and the increasingly numerous and equally impersonal relationships moderated through the online environment. Like information, the ability to procure services and establish relationships is now more diffuse than ever, and the need has arrived to manage due to abundance rather than stockpile due to scarcity.

In conjunction with the new routes to access, mechanisms of feedback represent the end of insulation of acquisitions functions from the rest of the service mission of the library. Increasingly automated mechanisms will loop feedback to or through acquisitions from a number of loci within the information universe.

One critical aspect of converting mechanized feedback into a dynamic element of service from acquisitions is knowing what feedback is available, what it implies about service, and how such feedback can ultimately improve the role of acquisitions within the library information and service environment. Online forms for reporting service outages and usage statistics automatically gathered through e-resource usage represent just two possibilities of feedback mechanisms that can inform the acquisitions process. Additional to informing acquisitions, increasing amounts of feedback will connect acquisitions to other processes and functions throughout the library.

The electronic systems used to manage acquisitions processes also provide an abundance of data about use. Of course, the very notion of "use" is problematic and the definition that sets parameters for what constitutes a use, or many uses, is itself a strategic decision. What is important to keep in mind is that what "use" is typically assumed to be indicative of is actually *usefulness* or, conversely, *need*. Therefore, care must be taken when reviewing any kind of use data to make sure that such data are meaningful within the context where they are gathered. One such initiative to improve this data is Counting Online Usage of NeTworked Electronic Resources (COUNTER). An initiative of international scope that includes publishers, vendors, and libraries, the ultimate goal of COUNTER is, basically, to establish "an agreed international set of standards and protocols governing the recording and exchange of online usage data" (COUNTER, n.d.). While usage was formerly dependent on circulation and in-house browse statistics, the ability to track and report online usage significantly increases knowledge of how resources are being used.

Automated feedback can provide a wealth of information to acquisitions. It is important that at every stage feedback informs acquisitions in such a way that decisions are made strategically. Feedback from the acquisitions and access processes must be incorporated in a contextual manner. Data generated from content management systems like usage statistics or inventory updates must inform decisions rather than dictate them. The fact that a title is out of print in paperback, for example, does not necessarily mean that the content is unavailable. Instead, it is imperative to engage feedback information in a critical way at the point where it reaches acquisitions.

Conclusion: Cycles of Service and Feedback

The cycle of access and feedback, which can be thought of as a continuous loop, is more advanced, granular, and pervasive than ever before. Given its position as a "broker," acquisitions acts from within this continuous loop of access and feedback actively and directly. Direct and active involvement with this cycle results in productive results and increased effectiveness, in terms of both better service and more efficient workflows. Such engagement by the entire acquisitions unit—whether it is composed of one or several practitioners—is also in keeping with the standard of practice to "establish practical and efficient methods for the conduct of his/her office" (ALCTS, 1994, Statement 11). In particular, the enhanced role of acquisitions as a service unit within both the *practice* and *mission* of the library is an effect of information derived from this loop.

Traditional notions of access and feedback were developed along the fixed channels that necessarily organized an analog information environment (Figure 4-5). Such channels make it difficult for acquisitions to act in a meaningful way.

A more useful model is one in which access and feedback are a continuous and ubiquitous loop comprising many sources (Figure 4-6). Like an expanded conception of formats, thinking about a granular, nuanced way of providing access and gathering feedback allows for a more relevant, malleable approach to

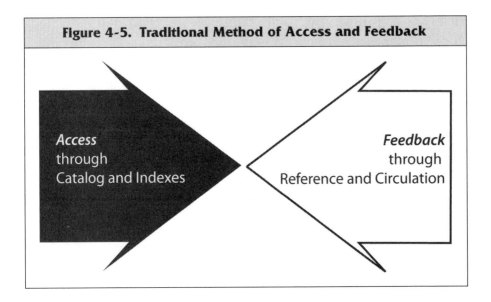

Figure 4-5. Traditional Method of Access and Feedback

Access through Catalog and Indexes

Feedback through Reference and Circulation

providing service while performing the familiar acquisitions functions.

It is clear that work in acquisitions is becoming more nuanced and complex. The work, once comprised chiefly of clerical tasks such as typing and filing, is "concentrating up," that is, requiring a well-developed skill set by more experienced staff. The capacity to automate processes combined with the necessity of working with formats that are increasingly complex to acquire and maintain results in an acquisitions function that is more technical and harder to define than ever before. Library usage can be tracked passively in a number of contexts, automating some of the content analysis and removing some of the supposition that have gone into previous collection development efforts. This level of data gathering may allow acquisitions to respond more immediately and directly to information needs. Surveys, distributed through a number of paths, have the potential to deal with concerns or ideas that relate directly to contemporary acquisitions functions. With more tasks that involve connecting both librarians and library users with content, the loop of establishing

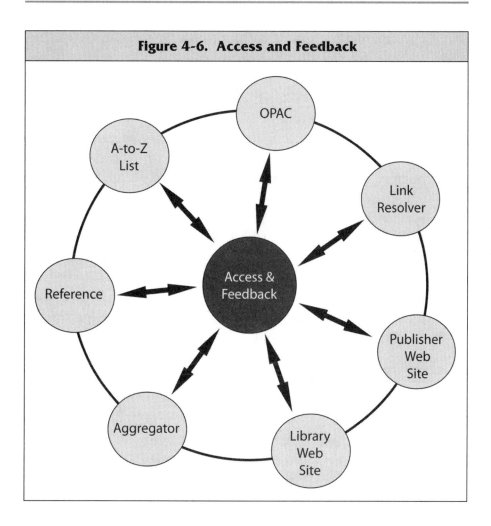

Figure 4-6. Access and Feedback

access and receiving feedback is a critical piece of the emerging acquisitions environment in the new information universe.

In general, the point-and-click culture of the information age has shaped a community of library users that are more aware of the acquisitions process, if less understanding of it. Therefore, service exposure—direct contact between acquisitions practitioners and the library user community—has increased for acquisitions practitioners. This is part of acquisitions' emerging role in the library. E-access has put a burden of technological implementation and deployment on acquisitions. Technology has in some cases led to unreal expectations that parallel the new possibilities that same technology has created. The idea that everything is available on the Internet makes anything less than instantaneous access seem like a delay. While a digital text might be delivered around the world in seconds, it might take days for a physical book to move across the state. The number of potential formats allows for more routes to access while also embedding more mechanisms of feedback. This environment creates the possibility of closer collaboration with other functional units within the library and better responsiveness to user needs. Meeting these new expectations can be done through collaboration within the library, university, and beyond. Reaching out to other acquisitions librarians with both counsel and assistance is an important principle of the profession (ALCTS, 1994, Statement 12), and takes on more importance as the information universe becomes increasingly large, access becomes increasingly complicated, and feedback becomes more ubiquitous.

References

ALCTS. 1994. "Statement on Principles and Standards of Acquisitions Practice." Acquisitions Section Ethics Task Force. Available: www.ala.org/ala/mgrps/divs/alcts/resources/collect/acq/acqethics.cfm (accessed October 15, 2009).

Anderson, Rick. 2007. "It's Not about the Workflow: Patron-Centered Practices for 21st-Century Serialists." *The Serials Librarian* 51, no. 3/4: 189–199.

Bosch, Stephen, Patricia Promis, and Chris Sugnet. 2005. *Guide to Licensing and Acquiring Electronic Information.* Lanham, MD: Scarecrow Press.

COUNTER. n.d. "About COUNTER." Available: www.project counter.org/ (accessed November 23, 2009).

Lopatin, Laurie. 2004. "Review of the Literature: Technical Services Redesign and Reorganization." *In Innovative Redesign and Reorganization of Technical Services: Paths for the Future and Case Studies,* edited by Radford Lee Eden. Westport, CT: Libraries Unlimited.

Chapter 5

Acquisitions in a New Paradigm

We live in a world where there is more and more information and less and less meaning.
—Jean Baudrillard (1994: 79)

Radical Strategies

It is an empirical fact that we live in an age of information overload. Vast amounts of information are available over the Internet, cable and satellite television, and satellite radio. Constant advances in computing and telecommunications make accessibility to this information at once easier and more mobile. The library, once an undisputed destination for the information seeker, is now just an intersection among a multiplicity of information pathways. The acquisitions professional no doubt faces a challenge in locating the right information in the most relevant format and establishing the necessary access. The use and, therefore, meaning of content is highly dependent on a combination of those factors. As the information universe becomes more complicated, the strategies employed to establish the requisite access to content necessarily become more complicated as well.

The most difficult part in an environment that is both increasingly complicated and always in flux is to establish a stable, meaningful strategy for acquisitions and the workflows that underpin the development of a likewise meaningful sphere of access. On the one hand, new technologies are re-creating available tools and opportunities for acquisitions on a continuous basis. On the other hand, the very flux that delivers options for purchase and access also means that successful strategies must be adaptable and therefore technology-neutral, to the extent possible. This paradox underlies all the challenges that contemporary practitioners of acquisitions must incorporate into their daily work.

Rather than reconfiguring old approaches to acquisitions only to reconfigure them again, practitioners must radicalize how they approach and perform acquisitions in the information age. This is, of course, easier said than done. While the constants in acquisitions—placing orders, receiving or establishing access to content, paying invoices—are what fundamentally define the practice beyond each individual library, the role of *the local* in developing a particular acquisitions function remains incredibly important. The variables that constitute the local also confound any attempt at a fully prescriptive methodology: Population served, information needs, collection focus, staffing levels, facilities, budget, and tax status are just a few variables operating at a local level that create a highly unique acquisitions situation at each library. What is obvious is that old approaches to acquisitions based on the primacy of paper will become increasingly inadequate to address the complex information needs of today's students and researchers.

What, then, does it mean to "radicalize" acquisitions? The most important step is to move definitively away from models that are based on the fixed linearity of process or standardization of information objects. Reflexively buying a book may not be an adequate strategy; engaging with collection development and access services to determine access needs, format availability, and new service models for delivering content to where the end users are is an approach on which to form a basis of acquisitions practice. While this is difficult to do, creatively engaging with the content goals and access issues within the context of a given library should inform any acquisitions strategy; service needs should drive acquisitions practices forward. The use of vendors when possible, technology when effective, and collaboration at each step of the way will leverage resources and streamline workflow. In the abstract, these are not new ideas. However, each one of these elements takes on new meaning and greater significance in technology-driven, always-online, interdisciplinary campus environments. The paradigm has shifted from a modern, mechanical information universe to a postmodern one that is often electronic and nonlinear.

The idea of "postmodern acquisitions" is not new, and has been a mode of thinking from early in the information age (Propas and Reich, 1995). However, a postmodern praxis within the realm of acquisitions is finally starting to reach its potential because of advances in technology coupled with changes in information-seeking culture. Immersed in an expanding, diversifying information universe, acquisitions professionals now find themselves facing a proliferation of formats, literally a vast field crowded with simulacra, as conceived by Baudrillard—copies without originals. Information exists as prints, reprints, photocopies, Web pages, scanned images, CDs, e-mails, streaming video, audio files—a host of formats endlessly propagating themselves through the information universe. Content can be reproduced and remixed across a variety of formats, distributed through an endless number of channels, and acted upon in infinite ways. The role of the original has not disappeared—far from it—but the original in terms of use (and therefore acquisitions) will be diminished. So, too, will the role of the item. Though acquisitions professionals will continue to buy items (and build some semblance of a traditional collection), the gathering of physical items is just one part of connecting library users with content. The acquisitions professional must not only be aware of or just take into account, but must actively incorporate new kinds of formats, unfamiliar objects, and challenging service models into their daily work.

The Future of Electronic Text

It is interesting to note that recent developments in e-book readers for the consumer market, such as the Amazon Kindle, Sony Reader, and iPod are changing the public perception of e-books. Most importantly, the popularity of mobile devices has overcome one of the great challenges in widespread e-book adoption, namely the e-novel. Amazon.com is attempting to address limits inherent in the first two models of the portable device by providing large-format or graphic-intensive publications with the release of its Kindle DX. Recently, Amazon expanded the content side of its business by making Kindle Reader software available for the iPod via iTunes, allowing Amazon to sell its proprietary Kindle e-books to iPod consumers. Into this mix, Google has already scanned million of books and is making those e-books in the public domain available for the Sony Reader (Snyder, 2009). Finally, textbooks are finally being released in e-book format to students, who could capitalize on portability, full-text searching, and other features possible in the e-book environment. This flurry of technological innovation and marketing signals a tipping point in the acceptance of e-books by a subset of the general public that is able to afford the expensive handheld hardware upon which this line of innovation has been developed. While e-journals in academia long ago started the shift from a print-based paradigm to one that recognizes and accepts a multiplicity of possible formats, such shifts in a more popular consumer interest in and use of electronic-based text signals a broader cultural shift in the adaptation of a multiplicity of formats.

Unlike the e-books intended for proprietary mobile devices carried by the technologically savvy reading public that mainstream corporations are targeting, the suppliers of academic e-books have, for the most part, focused their strategy on PC- and laptop-based access. By creating computer-delivered content, the academic library is able to take advantage of the college or university infrastructure to deliver content, including Wi-Fi networks, campus computer labs, and laptops of various manufacture. The university, on the other hand, can capitalize on e-books as a kind of distributed collection that can be accessed from anywhere, including classrooms and dorms. Disability services may also be able to leverage computer-delivered content in cases where the digital rights management (DRM) is not too restrictive. Demand in the consumer market for e-books signals that there may be a similar surge in popularity to follow in academic research. At the same time, the campus community's perception that the library (and especially the print monograph) is sacrosanct almost certainly has contributed to the slower adoption of the e-book in the academic library. Libraries, though, having long dealt with maintaining multiple formats for serials, are not in a position to duplicate monograph content in most cases. The movement toward e-publishing by mainstream publishers for a general audience has created an atmosphere where e-books are likely to be more accepted culturally.

The general popularity of e-books is being driven by many factors including technology and marketing. In the university, changing research practices and the expectations of incoming students are further driving demand. Within academic publishing, there is yet another factor. The economics of academic publishing are forcing publishers, and especially university presses (UPs), to find alternate models to continue to provide access to important academic research. With print production, storage, and distribution exerting pressure on the bottom lines of many UPs, these presses are forced to look to alternate means of publishing. The University of Michigan Press has announced plans for a two-year transition to a publishing model that emphasizes digital publishing over print, and which will put the university at the leading edge of academic monograph publishing (Jaschik, 2009[KF1]). It is doubtful that Michigan will be the last UP to make such a shift. Already, the University of Pittsburgh Press has made over 500 monographs available through their Digital Editions initiative (http://digital.library.pitt.edu/p/pittpress/). The titles offered by the University of Pittsburgh Press, mostly out of print at the time they are included in the initiative, have been made freely available in collaboration with the university's library system. While not as radical as the University of Michigan model, the University of Pittsburgh case clearly demonstrates a move to e-book format that is not entirely driven by the bottom line. Even more revolutionary is the recent decision by Utah State University Press to merge with the university's Merrill-Cazier Library, a plan that also includes making the press's publications available online via open access (Williams, 2009). Such a move presents an interesting example of a library shifting resources toward the actual publication of scholarly content rather than consumption of already published content. In still another route to academic e-books, MIT Press is making individual recent publications available for purchase through their Web site E-books at the MIT Press (http://mitpressebooks.mit.edu/). MIT most clearly represents a link to consumer consumption of e-books and provides a way to supplement print sales with electronic distribution of their own content. With UP titles, the recognized standard of academic excellence in monograph publishing, making determined steps toward long-term electronic publishing models, even those libraries reluctant to embrace e-content will likely have to grapple with issues associated with acquiring and providing access to e-books.

Diminishing Boundaries

If acquisitions is increasingly detached from *purchasing* and *ownership* in the strict sense of those terms while becoming more engaged directly with library users, the realignment of the acquisitions function spills over its traditional boundaries. If those in acquisitions are concerned with maintaining a more generalized and flexible sphere of access rather than building a solid physical collection, other library functions such as inter-library loan (ILL) and document delivery must be reevaluated as well. Though often separated into their own unit or incorporated into access services, a radicalization of acquisitions may well mean a shift in how these less permanent, patron-driven acquisitions are managed within the library. At the very least, the approval plan requires close coordination between collection development and acquisitions; however, the new information universe requires close collaboration with ILL and document delivery operations. In a matter of time, it may be difficult to distinguish the respective functions of these three processes enough to keep them all separate.

E-books, again, provide an interesting example. While a journal article not owned by the library may be supplied through a document delivery service, what about books in an electronic format: do these fall into ILL? Given the DRM surrounding e-books, it seems unlikely that they could be loaned outside of the institution or institutions (within a state system or consortium) that established access to the title to begin with. Since major e-book publishers already offer patron-driven purchase options, it seems more likely that instead of ILL, libraries might better satisfy user needs by simply allowing just-in-time purchasing of e-titles in many cases. While budgetary considerations (price per item and overall budget situation) will set de facto limits on patron selection, such a model not only provides immediate access but allows ongoing access for future library users. Developing such a service is clearly part of the acquisitions function: It is just another kind of book purchase. It is unlikely that all ILL and document delivery services will be immediately absorbed by acquisitions, and in many cases such a merge might not even make sense for a myriad of reasons. However, when looking at how information is being produced, distributed, and consumed, an approach to access should not impose distinctions from an old paradigm. E-books provide an example of a format for which it has become difficult to differentiate anticipatory acquisitions from just-in-time delivery. In the information age, such a sharp delineation needs to be abandoned in favor of a continuum. Instead of silos of responsibility, rigid and separate, functional boundaries must be fluid, permeable, and conducive to collaboration across the entire library.

Conclusion: Rhizomatic Acquisitions

Any acquisitions work today must be premised on an ever-growing amount of information, the changing nature of content, and an ability to be proactive and flexible in building the library's sphere of access. Deleuze and Guattari provide a fitting model for tracing information and acquiring formats in the new information age: "A system like this could be called a rhizome. A rhizome as a subterranean stem is absolutely different from roots and radicles" (1987: 6), typical of plants like ferns. Instead of providing a singular position or direction, "there are no points or positions in a rhizome, such as those found in a structure, root, or tree. There are only lines" (p. 8). Rather than fixed categories of content in fixed format traveling along linear chains in predetermined directions, a rhizomatic approach in acquisitions suggests moving in any and all directions to establish the sphere of access that allows library users to connect with the content that they seek. Rhizomatic lines represent the shortest routes, yet simultaneously imply free motion through the information universe. These lines are multidimensional; rhizomes do not dig in but grow outward in all directions.

This break, moving us from the *linear chains* of a past age to the *rhizomatic lines* of the information age, is not to be underestimated. The linear chains are, in fact, composed of segments, each segment in a sense forming a link of the chain—researcher to publisher or publisher to vendor, for example. The linear chains, though, are not the same as rhizomatic lines. Following Deleuze and Guattari, we are able at this point to "summarize the principal difference between rigid segmentarity and supple segmentarity. In the rigid mode, binary segmentarity stands on its own and is governed by great machines of direct binarization, whereas in the other [supple] mode, binaries result from 'multiplicities of n dimensions'" (1987: 212). Deleuze and Guattari, then, recognize the segmentary nature of the rigid lines, but note that they are functionally "governed by great machines of direct binarization." In the case of acquisitions, such "great machines" imposing this binarization might be traditional library practices; organizational rigidity of the unit, library, or university; or reluctance to consider new approaches. The end points in these cases of rigid segmentarity have always already been preestablished and are connected by fixed, predetermined lines—even if those lines are, in turn, composed of many segments. The flexibility, or suppleness, of the rhizomatic lines grants freedom—in terms of both the length and directionality of the lines. The "multiplicities of n dimensions" are opened up by the expanding number of formats, contingencies, and collaborations, allowing acquisitions to escape its own past limitations and fully engage in the possibilities of the information age.

The radicalization of acquisitions requires the dismantling of the preexisting conceptual apparatus of acquisitions—a fixed, rooted system—and reconstituting the assemblage as something at once less structured and more connected: "a multiplicity that necessarily changes in nature as it expands its connections" (Deleuze and Guattari, 1987: 8). As the universe expands and connections increase, routes to access and mechanisms of feedback increase, too. A fixed system is not in a position to respond, let alone be proactive to user expectations and needs. Rediscovering the universe as an assemblage of information, content, and formats, with all that might imply, rather than a structured system of exclusively physical entities to be bought and shelved—such a universe, where there are only lines, is the absolute key to acquisitions in the information age.

References

Baudrillard, Jean. 1994. *Simulacra and Simulation.* Translated by Sheila Faria Glaser. Ann Arbor: University of Michigan Press.

Deleuze, Gilles, and Felix Guattari. 1987. *A Thousand Plateaus: Capitalism and Schizophrenia.* Minneapolis: University of Minnesota Press.

Jaschik, Scott. 2009. "Farewell to the Printed Monograph." *Inside Higher Ed,* March 23. Available: www.insidehighered.com/news/2009/03/23/michigan (accessed November 23, 2009).

Propas, Sharon, and Vicky Reich. 1995. "Postmodern Acquisitions." *Library Acquisitions: Practice and Theory* 19, no. 1: 43–48.

Snyder, Chris. 2009. "Sony-Google E-book Deal a Win for ePub, Openness." *Epicenter,* March 19. Available: http://www.wired.com/epicenter/2009/03/sony-google-e-b/ (accessed June 25, 2009).

Williams, Patrick. 2009. "Utah State University Press Merges with Merrill-Cazier Library." Utah State University. Available: www.usu.edu/ust/index.cfm?article=40291 (accessed November 23, 2009).

Selected Resources

Conferences

The Acquisitions Institute at Timberline Lodge
http://libweb.uoregon.edu/ec/aitl/

This small conference is held annually at the Timberline Lodge on Mount Hood, Oregon.

Annual Charleston Conference: "Issues in Book and Serials Acquisition"
www.katina.info/conference/generalinfo.php

This large conference is held in Charleston, South Carolina, in early November. The conference includes participation from publishers, vendors, and librarians.

Electronic Resources and Libraries
www.electroniclibrarian.org/erlwiki/ER%26L

This relatively new annual conference was created to provide a forum for all aspects of e-resources in libraries.

North American Serials Interest Group (NASIG) Annual Conference
www.nasig.org/conference_registration.cfm

The NASIG conference focuses on serials and other recurring resources. The conference changes location every year.

E-mail Lists

ACQNET-L
http://lists.ibiblio.org/mailman/listinfo/acqnet-l

This list carries all kinds of acquisitions-related information, including questions, surveys, and job announcements.

AUTOACQ-L
www.lsoft.com/scripts/wl.exe?SL1=AUTOACQ-L&H=LISTSERV .ND.EDU

This e-mail list is for "acquisitions automation issues."

Electronic Resources in Libraries (ERIL-L)
http://listserv.binghamton.edu/archives/eril-l.html

The ERIL-L e-mail list is for posting questions or information about electronic resources of all kinds.

LIBLICENSE-L
www.library.yale.edu/~llicense/index.shtml

This list focuses on issues about and related to licensing resources for libraries.

Online Courses

Fundamentals of Acquisitions (FOA)
Chicago: Association for Library Collections and Technical Services
www.ala.org/ala/mgrps/divs/alcts/confevents/upcoming/webcourse/ foacquisitions.cfm

This instructor-facilitated, four-week online course covers the basics of acquisitions.

Fundamentals of Electronic Resource Acquisitions (FERA)
Chicago: Association for Library Collections and Technical Services

www.ala.org/ala/mgrps/divs/alcts/confevents/upcoming/webcourse/
foelectronic.cfm

This instructor-facilitated, four-week course specifically focuses
on the acquisition of electronic resources.

Serials

Against the Grain
Charleston, SC: Against the Grain
www.against-the-grain.com

Published six times a year, ATG covers a wide range of topics,
including publishing, vending, collection development, and
acquisitions librarianship.

Charleston Conference Proceedings
Santa Barbara: Libraries Unlimited
www.abc-clio.com

The Proceedings constitute an annual volume of presentations
from the Charleston Conference.

Journal of Electronic Resource Librarianship (continues The Acquisitions Librarian)
New York: Routledge
www.informaworld.com/smpp/title~db=all~content=t792303957

Representing a broader shift in library collections, the recent
title change and content coverage of this journal demonstrates a prevailing trend in libraries. Not limited solely to the
acquisition of e-resources, the coverage of this "new" journal
is more holistic.

Library Collections, Acquisitions, and Technical Services
Oxford: Pergamon Press
www.elsevier.com/wps/find/journaldescription.cws_home/293/
description#description

LCATS publishes research-based articles from a breadth of international contributors.

Library Resources & Technical Services
Chicago: Association for Library Collections and Technical Services
www.ala.org/alcts/lrts

The quarterly journal of the Association for Library Collections and Technical Services (ALCTS), *LRTS* includes articles on acquisitions but tends to focus more on cataloging.

The Serials Librarian
New York: Routledge
www.informaworld.com/smpp/title~db=all~content=t792306962

This journal covers all aspects of continuing resources, including both practical and theoretical articles.

Technical Services Quarterly
New York: Routledge
www.informaworld.com/smpp/title~content=t792306978~link=cover

The primary focus of this journal is on automation and computing in the context of technical services.

Web Sites

AcqWeb
www.acqweb.org

This site compiles information and resources relating to the practice of acquisitions. Recently redesigned, the new version features several blogs.

Against the Grain
www.against-the-grain.com

This Web site was created in association with the *Against the Grain* journal. The site features announcements, blogs, and some full-text content from *ATG*.

NASIG
www.nasig.org

This is the Web site of the North American Serials Interest Group.

UKSG
www.uksg.org

This is the Web site of the United Kingdom Serials Group.

Index

Page numbers followed by the letter "f" indicate figures; those followed by the letter "s" indicate sidebars; those followed by the letter "d" indicate definitions.

A

AACR2, 84

Access
  controls, 92
  models of, 89f, 102f, 103f
  potential, 88s
  process, 18, 19s, 46, 54, 78, 91,
      100
  routes to (*see* Routes to
      access)
  strategy, 47–50

Acquisitions
  alternate modes of, 48s–49s
  conception of, ix, 6
  environment, 8, 103–104
  functional organization of, 87
  as an item-based function, 86f
  mission of, x, 39
  organization of, 87
  process
    and automation, 102
    and electronic systems, 100

and feedback, 100
and function, 24, 87
in general, xii, 15, 17, 17s,
    20, 41s, 46, 50, 71, 76,
    103, 113
and the ILS, 42, 94
item-based, ix, 7, 15, 53,
    62s, 70
and linearity, 10, 19–20, 25,
    108
local, 85
and streamlining, 93
practitioners (*see also*
    Acquisitions:
    professionals)
and access, 91, 101
and assumptions, 53
and containers, 25
and contingencies, 18
and facilitating access, 45
and feedback, 101
and information, 5

ONIX-PL, 78
Online vendor databases, x, 28,
  29d, 34–35, 60, 67, 92, 93
  as an ERMS, 95, 98
Open access, 45, 46d, 49s, 75–76
Ordering, process of
  and access, 78, 93
  and approval plans, 34 (*see
    also* Approval plans)
  and the ILS, 94
  and items, 78
  and online vendors, 35
  and potential access, 88s
  responsibility for, x, 16s, 20,
    108
  structuring, 77
Ordering systems, 67, 93. *See also*
  Online vendor databases
Orders, for content
  approvals, 95 (*see also*
    Approval plans)
  and the archive, 73
  canceling, 20, 27s, 76
  claiming, 20, 24, 30s, 42, 93,
    96
  and discounts, 25
  and EDI, 42d
  for electronic resources, 95
  and the ILS, 94
  mail, 46, 91
  maintaining, 94
  managing, 94
  online, 29d, 67, 69, 94
  paid, 74
  paper, 10
  placing (*see* Ordering)
  and process, 77, 78

receipt (*see* Orders: receiving)
receiving, ix, x, 16s, 20, 47,
  75, 88s, 93, 94, 108
requests, 23
standing, 17s
status, 30s, 35
submission (*see* Ordering)
and tracking, 78, 88s, 94
unfulfilled (*see* Orders:
  claiming)

P
Paper, primacy of, 24
Paradigm shift, 3, 4, 6–7, 10, 11,
  18
Patron-driven purchasing, 113
Payment
  with credit cards (*see* Credit
    cards; P-cards)
  and electronic systems, 92
  and the ILS, 42, 94
  terms, 27s
  to vendors, 40, 42 (*see also*
    Credit cards; P-cards;
    World Wide Web:
    retailers)
P-cards, 42d, 42–43. *See also*
  Credit cards
Physical processing, 27s, 28, 28d,
  36s
Postmodern, 8, 18, 109
Preservation, 70
Principles. *See* "Statement on
  Principles and Standards of
  Acquisitions Practice"
Print-on-demand, 77
Procurement, x, xi, 21, 25, 54

About the Author

Jesse Holden is Coordinator of Technical Services at Millersville University in Pennsylvania. Previously he was the ordering librarian in the Acquisitions Department at the Stanford University Libraries and the acquisitions librarian at the Stanford Law Library. He was formerly an instructor for the ALCTS online course Fundamentals of Acquisitions and is currently an instructor for the ALCTS online course Fundamentals of Electronic Resource Acquisitions. He is editor of the column "Acquisitions Archaeology," which is featured in the journal *Against the Grain*. He earned his MLIS degree from San Jose State University.